Sir Samuel Ferguson

The Remains of St. Patrick, Apostle of Ireland, the Confessio

and Epistle to Coroticus

Sir Samuel Ferguson

The Remains of St. Patrick, Apostle of Ireland, the Confessio and Epistle to Coroticus

ISBN/EAN: 9783337323820

Printed in Europe, USA, Canada, Australia, Japan

Cover: Foto ©Lupo / pixelio.de

More available books at **www.hansebooks.com**

THE REMAINS OF St. PATRICK,

APOSTLE OF IRELAND.

THE CONFESSIO AND EPISTLE TO COROTICUS.

Translated into English Blank Verse,

WITH

A DISSERTATION ON THE PATRICIAN DOCUMENTS CONTAINED IN THE "TRIAS THAUMATURGA" AND "BOOK OF ARMAGH," ETC.

BY

SIR SAMUEL FERGUSON, LL.D.,

President of the Royal Irish Academy.

DUBLIN:
SEALY, BRYERS & WALKER,
94, 95 & 96 MIDDLE ABBEY STREET.

LONDON:
GEORGE BELL & SONS,
5 YORK STREET, COVENT GARDEN.

1888.

Printed by
SEALY, BRYERS & WALKER,
94, 95 & 96 Middle Abbey Street.
Dublin.

THE PATRICIAN DOCUMENTS

BY

Sir Samuel Ferguson, LL.D.

THE CONFESSIO AND EPISTLE TO COROTICUS.

The Publishers of this cheap edition of Sir Samuel Ferguson's works beg to announce that they have taken steps to ensure the copyright in America and elsewhere. and that any infringement of it will be punishable by law.

I Dedicate this Book
TO
FOUR FRIENDS, MUCH ESTEEMED AND VALUED BY ME
AS WELL AS BY HIM WHOM I DEPLORE.

THE ARCHBISHOP OF DUBLIN
AND
THE BISHOP OF MEATH,
WHOSE APPRECIATION OF THIS, ALMOST THE LATEST WORK
OF MY HUSBAND'S LIFE, HAS ENCOURAGED ME
TO RE-PUBLISH IT;
AND ALSO TO
THE BISHOP OF DOWN, CONNOR AND DROMORE
AND
THE REV. ROBERT KING,
WHOSE LEARNED AND DELIGHTFUL WORKS HAVE INTERESTED
ME FROM EARLY YOUTH IN THE HISTORY OF OUR
IRISH SAINTS.
TO THEIR
LONG AND TRIED FRIENDSHIP, AS WELL AS TO THEIR
WRITINGS, I AM INDEBTED FOR MUCH OF THE
HAPPINESS OF MY LIFE.

M. C. FERGUSON.

20 NORTH GREAT GEORGE'S STREET, DUBLIN,
August, 1888.

INTRODUCTION.

I HAVE to thank the Council of the Royal Irish Academy for the permission kindly accorded to me to re-publish my husband's last contribution to the Transactions of that learned body, of which he was President at the time of his death.

The Patrician Documents was the title that Sir Samuel Ferguson gave to these papers; they consisted of his translation into English blank verse, of the *Confessio* and the *Coroticus Epistle*, which are admitted by scholars to be authentic writings of St. Patrick himself, and to have come down to us from the fifth century of our era. The *Patrician Documents* included dissertations upon these, and on the lives published by Colgan in his *Trias Thaumaturga*, as well as an examination into the collections in the Book of Armagh and elsewhere, not accessible to Colgan, who wrote in the middle of the seventeenth century.

To the ordinary reader without pretension to scholarship, nor specially interested in the controversies of these early days, the chief attraction of these writings of St. Patrick will be the revelation they afford of the man himself; of his character, motives, and springs of action; of what he aimed at and what achieved. They furnish what may be fairly described as the great missionary Saint's autobiography.

His family were of good condition. "I was born noble, my father a *Decurio*." That father, Calphurn, was not only a Roman official, but was also an ecclesiastic, a deacon, the son of a presbyter, Potitus, and resided on a farm at "Bannow of Tabernia," which the narrative implies to have been in insular Britain, and within the Roman Province, bounded by the wall of Agricola, between the estuaries of the Clyde and Forth. The wall restored in the second century by the Emperor Antoninus Pius, was the defence of the civilized and christianized Britons against the incursions of the Picts and Scots.

The birthplace of St. Patrick has not been recorded by himself, but later biographers state it to have been called Nemthor, otherwise Ail-clyde. Ail-clyde has been identified with Dumbarton on the Clyde, the western terminus of the Roman Wall. Saint Patrick tells us that he was carried captive to Ireland, in the sixteenth year of his age, doubtless in one of the piratical expeditions of the Pagan Scoti, or Irish, and was there sold into slavery. It was his hapless fate to herd the cattle of his master on the mountain of Slemish, in the present county of Antrim. Here, friendless and alone, he passed six years in want and hardship, but with leisure for reflection. Although in his boyhood a member of a Christian family, the future Apostle of the Irish was ignorant of God, and estranged from his Commandments; but now the Lord, pitying his youth and ignorance, visited and consoled him, turning his heart to Him, so that he attained the "touch and apprehension" of his God, and was prepared to confess Him before men. Saint Patrick speaks of himself as unlearned and ignorant, and the debased Latin in which he writes—which was common at the time in Western Europe—intermixed as it is with

Irish idioms, makes his language in many places very obscure; yet he was versed in Holy Scripture, and quotes freely from the sacred writings. His humility, his grateful acknowledgments of the Divine mercy bestowed on him, and his earnest zeal for the salvation of souls, are expressed repeatedly in his *Confessio*.

> "With fear and reverence,
> Faithful in heart and uncomplainingly,
> I serve this people, to whom the charity
> Of Christ assigns me for my rest of life,
> If I be worthy, that with humble heart
> And truthful lips, I teach it, in the faith
> And measure of the Holy Trinity.
>   Behoves me, therefore, fearless of rebuke
> Or danger, that I do set forth the gift
> And everlasting consolation
> Of God; and fearlessly declare His name
> Abroad where'er I be; . . .
>   But, herding daily here,
> And often in the day saying my prayers,
> Daily there more and more did grow in me
> The fear of God. And holy fear and faith
> Increased in me, that in a single day
> I've said as many as a hundred prayers,
> And in the night scarce fewer; so that oft
> In woods and on the mountain I've remained,
> And risen to prayer before daylight, through snow,
> Through frost, through rain, and yet I took no ill,
> Nor was there in me then aught slow as now,
> For then the Spirit of God within me burned,"

He tells that in his childhood he had been estranged from God, and remained in death and unbelief, till chastised by hunger, nakedness, and enforced toil in Ireland.

> "Yet these were rather boons to me, because
> So chastened by the Lord, I now am made
> What once was far from me, that I should care
> Or labour for the weal of others
> Who then took no thought even for myself."

At last the opportunity of escape presented itself. It was borne in on his mind that he should leave the master whose bondman he had been. Dreams, visions, or an inward voice, in which Saint Patrick firmly believed, and throughout his career frequently referred to, whispered that he should see his home again.

> "I heard the voice,
> And this is what it said: 'Behold, thy ship
> Is ready,' but the ship lay nowise near,
> But nigh two hundred miles off, and where I
> Had never been before, and no man knew.
> So, thereupon, I turned myself to flight,
> Leaving the man whom I had served six years,
> And by the help of God, who showed me well
> The way to go, nought dreading, found the ship."

In this vessel he embarked, and after trying experiences, during a journey of sixty days, found himself "once more amongst the Britons," with his family, who received him with affectionate warmth, and entreated him never again to leave them.

The desire to win souls to God, and in especial those of the people among whom he had lived as a slave, overpowered in the missionary saint the love of home and friends and personal ease. He was prepared to endure persecutions, and for the good of others forfeit his "own patrician grade." That privilege of birth he was ready to renounce for the benefit of others. "What," he exclaims,

> "Was it then without God's promises,
> Or in the body only, that I came
> To Ireland? Who compelled me? Who me bound
> In spirit that I should no more behold
> Kindred or early friend? Whence came the sense
> Inspiring me with pity for the race
> That once were my own captors?"

Saint Patrick has himself answered these questions. He believed that he was specially summoned to his missionary work in Ireland in a dream which he thus records:

> "In a night vision, I beheld a man
> Coming as 'twere from Ireland. Victor he.
> Innumerable letters bore he; one
> He gave to me to read. I read one line,
> 'The voices of the Irish,' so it ran.
> And while I read methought I heard the cry
> Of them that by the wood of Focluth dwell,
> Beside the western ocean, saying thus,
> 'Come, holy youth, and walk amongst us. Come!'
> All with one voice. It touched me to the heart,
> And I could read no more, and so awoke.
> Thank God at last who, after many years,
> Has given to them according to their cry!"

Like the great Apostle of the Gentiles, he, of the Irish, "was not disobedient unto the heavenly vision." Saint Patrick also resembled St. Paul in the assured conviction that he was divinely appointed to be a witness for Christ, called on to preach Him among the heathen. "*I* send thee," was the commission of Jesus, "to open their eyes, and to turn them from darkness to light." The parallel is very close. The conversion of both these apostles was independent of the intervention of human instrumentality. These eminently successful evangelists unhesitatingly obeyed their call to missionary work, and could alike exclaim, "I do not frustrate the grace of God."

> "Therefore unwearied thanks I render Him
> Who kept me faithful in temptation's hour,
> That I to-day should live to offer up
> Myself a living sacrifice to Him,
> My Saviour, my Preserver. Well may I
> Say, Lord, what am I? or my calling what?
> That with such favour, with such aid divine,
> Thou hast environed and uplifted me,
> As daily I amongst the Gentiles rise

> Higher and higher, whilst I glorify
> Thy name where'er I be. Whate'er befalls,
> Happy or wretched, good or ill, the same
> I deem, and equally for it thakn Thee
> With thanks perpetual, for that Thou hast shown
> Him, the most sure, indubitable One,
> In whom I may believe for ever, Him
> Who will for ever hear me. So, too, I,
> In these last days, though ignorant, may dare
> Address me to a work so holy—good,
> So wondrous, as may even make parity
> 'Twixt me and them, who, He Himself foretold,
> Should bear His joyful message, witnessing
> Him to all people, ere the world should end."

This is the true missionary spirit: "Freely ye have received, freely give," and was fully evidenced in Saint Patrick's life and work. "Lo I still spend, and still will further spend, happy if He, who can, shall yet allow that for your sakes I even may spend my soul."

The same yearning love for his converts which characterised St. Paul, marks also the personality of Saint Patrick.

> "But never, never let me lose the flock
> He pastures by me in earth's outland here!
> God grant me that! and that I persevere
> In faithful witness to my journey's end."

And yet his heart often turned with longing to the friends from whom he was separated and to his father's house. "Sure 'twere sweet to see one's country and one's kin again." "I declare in truth," adds Saint Patrick, at the close of the *Confessio*, "before my God and His most holy angels, that I never had any object, save the gospel and His promises, for returning to that people from whom so hardly I escaped before."

> "And now beseech all them that do believe
> And fear the Lord, whoe'er they be, shall deign
> Look on this writing or receive the same,
> Which, sinner Patrick, I the much-unlearned,

> Have writ in Ireland, that no man may say
> My ignorance it was dictated aught,
> If any aught of good be therein seen,
> Such as may pleasure God; but rather deem,
> For certain, that it doth proceed from Him.
> And this is my confession ere I die."

The *Epistle to Coroticus*, which bears internal evidence of having been written by the author of the *Confessio*, has also been translated by Sir Samuel Ferguson into English blank verse. It is an indignant letter, written to a British prince of that name, who had sold into slavery, to the apostate Picts and Scots, certain captives, Christian men and women, for whose release the writer earnestly pleads. "It also," observes its translator, "like the *Confessio*, uses some expressions not consonant to the Latin, but to the Celtic idiom, as though the writer in both conceived his thoughts in some form of Celtic speech and expressed them in Latin. . . . In the *Confessio* the inner nature of the writer is seen throughout. In the *Coroticus* he is seen in his relations with an external world of wrong and suffering, against which he struggles with the grief and indignation any pastor might experience whose flock had been made the prey of lawless violence. Still there breathes through its reproaches and words of technical objurgation a lofty sentiment and energy of imagination which would make any prose translation inadequate to its full reproduction."

This, the oldest document in British history, shows in fresh light the noble, fearless, yet tender and loving personality of the great Apostle of Ireland. He thus concludes his letter:

> "I now beseech His servant, whosoe'er
> Shall set him forth to be the carrier
> Of these my letters, that he suffer none
> Abstract them privily, but have them read

> Before all peoples publicly, yea, read
> In presence of Coroticus himself.
> May God inspire them that they think at length
> Of Him, and, even late although it be,
> Repent them of the wickedness they've done.
> Manslayers of their brethren in the Lord
> They have been. May they yet repent, and free
> Their captive baptized women; so that yet
> They may themselves deserve to live in God
> And have eternal safety. Now be peace
> To Father, Son, and Holy Ghost. Amen."

Sir Samuel Ferguson, in his Preface, gives the reason for his selection of the form which he adopted in these translations. "A literal prose translation," he writes, "reflecting all the discontinuances and hesitancies of the original, would indeed repel most readers from the necessary task of collecting the general sense and bearing of the whole piece, and would scarcely at all realize the intense pervading fervour and, however obstructed in its utterance, the characteristic effusiveness of the original. To convey these in English prose would require something more in the nature of a free paraphrase, which would not be an acceptable constituent in a critical essay. What appears to me a less repellent and more exact form in which to present the piece, as combining literalness with suitability for the expression of that fervent and effusive feeling which underlies its broken Latinity, is a close version in English blank verse." How he has performed the difficult task to which he applied himself, I shall leave to others to state. In the touching funeral address delivered by the Archbishop of Dublin in St. Patrick's Cathedral, on the 12th August, 1886, His Grace, Lord Plunket, said, with reference to this work:

"I have spoken of our dear brother as a SCHOLAR. He was a man of general culture and of varied learning; but, as we all know, his chief eminence was attained in the department of antiquarian research. .. I have spoken of him as a POET. ... He had the passion and fire of the genuine poet, tempered at the same time by great tenderness and purity. ... There is, however, among his poems, or rather his poetical translations, one legacy which we who meet together in this cathedral ought specially to prize—I mean the last paper which he read before the Royal Irish Academy upon '*Patrician Documents*'—a paper containing a wonderfully beautiful translation of those works which all learned men attribute, as genuine, to the great founder of Christianity in this land. This translation is one that we must all treasure; and we should all thank God that, before our dear brother was taken from us, he left us such a legacy."

At the first stated general meeting of the Royal Irish Academy held subsequently to Sir Samuel Ferguson's decease, his successor in the presidential chair, the Rev. Dr. Haughton, F.T.C.D., observed, in reference to this work: "In the department of antiquities, we have had from our late president the translation of the Patrician Documents into his own graceful and attractive Anglo-Irish, of which he was so complete a master—a translation which must draw and win students of other branches of knowledge who would otherwise have cared little for Saint Patrick and his literary memorials. ... He (Sir Samuel Ferguson) devoted his life to the effort to win for Ireland, if possible, both in literature and science, the first place. His ideas are perhaps best expressed in his own words:

"——'The man aspires
To link his present with his country's past,
And live anew in knowledge of his sires.

No rootless colonist of alien earth,
Proud, but of patient lungs and pliant limb;
A stranger in the land that gave him birth,
The land a stranger to itself and him.'"

b

On the same occasion Robert Atkinson, Esq., LL.D., Secretary of Council, observed of Sir Samuel Ferguson: "The love for antiquarian studies animated him down to the last year of his life, from his first paper, published in January, 1838, to his last work on the 'Patrician Documents,' 1885—a work which gives us the measure alike of the intimacy of his acquaintance with the story of Ireland's Apostle and of his mastery over the riches and beauty of the English tongue."

About the same time the Bishop of Meath addressed the following letter to the editor of a Dublin newspaper:—

SIR SAMUEL FERGUSON'S LATEST WORK.

TO THE EDITOR OF THE IRISH TIMES.

SIR,—In echoing the sentiments of deep regret you have well expressed on Sir Samuel Ferguson's death, I wish to take the opportunity of calling the attention of the public to what I believe was the last literary work of his life—it is the translation into verse of the "Remains of St. Patrick." It gives, in a most remarkable manner, a more comprehensible and a juster representation, especially of the "Confession," than any prose translation could do.

It is, so far as I know, accessible only in the Transactions of the Royal Irish Academy. May I express a hope that that learned and scientific body will allow this most remarkable work to be published by itself in such a manner as to become available for use to the general public.

Yours, etc.,

C. P. MEATH.

It may be of interest to mention in connection with this, almost the latest literary work of his life, that Sir Samuel Ferguson's thoughts more than half a century before, had been directed to the history and experiences of Saint Patrick. In his early manhood the personality of the great Apostle of Ireland had impressed itself on his imagination, and in a story written, almost in his boyhood, *The Return of Claneboy*, and recently re-published in the first Series of his *Hibernian Nights' Entertainments*, the characters introduced are taken to the mountain of Slemish, and discourse of the captivity of the Saint, and its results.

A youthful scion of the house of O'Neill, accompanied by his tutor, is described as having forded the river Bann, and ridden forward in advance of his attendants towards the hills to the north of Connor; here O'Neill pulls rein, and addresses his companion:

"Ho, Loughlin, these are brave mountains! they look not like other hills; they are broad-swelling, and rolled together like a wave of the sea, or an army of good warriors! How name you that great one that rises over all like the ship among the waves, or the king's presence on the ridge of battle?"

"That," answered the Erenach, "is the great Mount Slemish. We shall be on its summit ere sunset, and I shall then show thee the whole land of Dalaradia from Mourne to Rathlin."

They pursued their way along the vale of Broughshane through thick woods that for a time hid everything else from their view, and were almost under the western precipices of Slemish before they beheld its huge wedge-like bulk piercing the blue sky overhead.

* * * *

Rounding the southern shoulder of Slemish, our travellers came upon a fountain, springing out of the green sward, beside a great stone which seemed to have come down at one bound from the brow of the precipice above, for it was sunk halfway in the earth, and overhanging, as if arrested by the depth of the first dint it had made in the soil.

Under this they halted.

* * * *

"Is not this a strange and solemn scene, Prince?" said the Erenach. "This lonely hollow at our feet, this black rock on which we stand, these wooded wildernesses all around, and that solitary well-spring in the midst, rising unwearied and silent, and sliding down the same smooth path from century to century! Knowest thou who wandered amid these woods and mountains, climbed those rocks, and drank of these blessed waters eight centuries ago?"

"I know not," said O'Neill, "unless perhaps a herd of wild boars or a troop of wolves."

"Oh, holy and blessed Patrick!" exclaimed the Erenach, "was it for this that the visions came to thee by night, and the voice of the unborn infants of Erin crying out of the forest for redemption, that the scene of thy prayer and fasting should be deserted and forgotten, that the people of thy choice should be made vagabond like Cain!"

"Nay," said O'Neill, "I knew not that the good saint had been a mountaineer of Dalaradia."

"Knowest thou not the song of Fiech of Sliebtha?" said the Erenach.

"From beginning to end," answered O'Neill; "I learned it of Callough Moyle, my grandfather's bard."

"What says he in his 16th and 17th stanzas?" said his preceptor.

O'Neill repeated the Irish of the following:—

"By the fountain that never knows drought or decrease,
He nightly sang an hundred psalms
In service of the King of Angels,
Then went he to sleep on the bare rock,
His covering round about a damp mantle,
His pillow of rest, the bark of the forest tree."

"And what sayeth his own epistle, when he tells how the love of God increased within him day by day in his captivity?" questioned the Erenach.

O'Neill paused for an instant to recollect, then repeated the passage—"Etiam in sylvis et monte manebam, et ante lucem excitabar ad orationem, per nivem, per gelu, per pluviam ; et nihil mali sentiebam, neque ulla pigritia erat in me."

"You look now upon these woods," cried the Erenach "this is that mountain, and yonder well-spring is that fount! Hear me, Prince, we stand on the most blessed ground in Europe, in the cradle of the Church, in the nursery of kingdoms, in the very womb and navel of western Christendom! for here it was, even in this wild and lonely rock of Slemish, that God raised up the reclaimer of the Pagan, and here I make a vow, and I call these hills and waters and these eternal rocks to be perpetual witness against me, that through good and evil, through honour and dishonour, through life and death, I will devote myself to the sacred cause of this thy thrice blessed land's recovery."

O'Neill stood apart, astonished and in silence, while the other knelt and prayed ; and neither spoke, till at length the Erenach having risen, the Prince turned himself again to the wonders at his feet.

Fifty years and upwards of a studious life had passed ere Sir Samuel Ferguson again turned his mind to the elucidation of Saint Patrick's history. How he worked and how he laboured that he might preserve the story of the dear ancestral Island, this book as well as many other products of his pen will testify. In the prose portion of this work he entered fully into critical inquiries as to the date and credibility of the various lives of St. Patrick which have come down to us from the sixth and subsequent centuries.

"These Secondary Evidences," he writes, "consist of the seven lives published by Colgan in his *Trias Thauma-*

turga, and of the collections in the Book of Armagh not accessible to him, supplemented by the valuable matter lately restored to them from the Royal Library of Brussels, by the Rev. Edward Hogan, in his 'Documenta de Sco. Patricio.' "

The earliest of these is known as the "Fiacc Metrical Life," certainly later in date than A.D. 565, as it alludes to the abandonment of Tara, which had been for some 600 years the seat of regal power in Ireland, but was deserted in the sixth century after Christ. It is written in Irish, "a very archaic example of the language, and is composed in rhymed verse." This Sir Samuel has rendered in couplets, following the text and translation, printed by Dr. Whitley Stokes, in his "Goidelica."

Lives II., III., IV. in the *Trias Thaumaturga*, ascribed by Colgan, to Patrick junior, Benignus, and Eleran the Wise, bear internal evidence of being of later composition than the *Annotations of Tirechan*, in the Book of Armagh. This MS., now in the Library of Trinity College, Dublin, is a small vellum quarto, the writing of which is ascribed to Ferdomnach, who died A.D. 844. In its pages he requests the prayers of its readers—*Pro ferdomnacho orés*. The manuscript is inferred on other grounds to have been penned in the year 807. The notices it contains of St. Patrick are considered by that eminent scholar, Dr. Reeves, now Bishop of Down and Connor, to be the oldest and most authentic now in existence. The Book of Armagh is not only the source from whence other biographies borrow, but it has preserved earlier traditions and preceding literature; such, for example, as the so-called *Dicta Patricii*, and the *Confessio* which Tirechan quotes as the writing of St. Patrick himself, calling it *scriptio sua*. The same venerable manuscript contains also what is known as the

Muirchu Life. Of this portion of the Book of Armagh, some chapters are missing; these have been recently recovered from a vellum MS. life of St. Patrick, in the Royal Library at Brussels, which as mentioned above, has been carefully compared by the Rev. E. Hogan, S.J., with the Armagh Codex, as it proved to be a perfect twelfth century copy of the *Muirchu* Life in the Book of Armagh, and to contain the missing chapters from the older manuscript.

The fifth and sixth Lives, ascribed by Colgan to Probus and Jocelyn, date from about the tenth century, and yield in interest and value to the seventh Life known as the *Tripartite* with its duplicate in Irish. "This," writes Sir Samuel Ferguson, "is the most copious repertory of all; and from the fact that the first elements of almost all its matter may be found in the Book of Armagh, either recorded at length or indicated in the rough index to names of persons and places at the end of *Tirechan* in that collection, there can be little doubt that whatever be the date of its compilation in its present form, most of its substance is drawn from traditions, which were current before the compilation of the Armagh Codex. It may, therefore, be of an authority equal to that of any of the antecedent Lives."

Sir Samuel Ferguson enters at length upon the interesting yet complex inquiries suggested by these "Lives" and "Documents," and discusses their points of agreement and of difference as amongst one another, as well as their date and comparative value, and points out the immense difficulty of attempted reconcilements of the details given in these "Secondary Evidences" with the facts recorded by Saint Patrick himself in the "Primary Evidences"—namely, the *Confessio* and *Epistle to Coroticus*. He has marshalled these authorities with the utmost clearness of statement, the result, no doubt, of his legal training, wide knowledge of the subject, love of truth, and candour of mind. He thus sums up his labours:

"The evidences, it is believed, are here somewhat more systematically marshalled. ... To judge of these elements of opinion, it was necessary that both sets of evidence should be before the reader, and they are now, it is believed for the first time, presented in one catenation."

The prose portion of his work is, in short, a judicial summing up of evidence by a clear and competent judge. But the reader must undertake the responsibilities of the intelligent juryman. This is a task from which some may shrink, and for such it may be desirable to attempt some elucidation of these disputed points.

The reader, familiar with the legends derived from later sources and the controversies grounded thereon, as to whether Saint Patrick visited Gaul, Lerins, Rome, &c., and received his commission from St. Germanus of Auxerre, or Bishop Amathorex, or Pope Celestine himself, will do well to observe that the *Confessio* and *Epistle to Coroticus* afford no data on which to decide these questions. They contain but a casual allusion to Gaul and none whatsoever to Italy, nor are any of the above-named personages alluded to. The writer dwells, in the *Confessio*, on his attachment to his Irish converts and unwillingness to leave them, even although

> "'Twere sweet
> To see one's country and one's kin again;
> Or farther yet proceeding, even to Gaul,
> To see the brethren, and the faces see
> Of my Lord's saints, God knows I were right glad!
> But in the Spirit am bound; and He declares
> I were God's recreant did I leave them so.
> Moreover, truth it is, I would not lose
> The fruit of all my labour, well begun.
> Yet 'tis not I determine, but my Lord,
> He who commanded I should hither come,

> That here I should fulfil my rest of days
> In serving them, and so methinks I shall."

So that it seems almost implied that the apostle did *not* elect to leave Ireland, and this is the only passage in these, his undoubted writings, in which he refers to the possibility of a visit to Gaul. But he does refer to a second captivity subsequent to the six years of slavery from which he escaped in the ship which bore him from Ireland. He minutely describes the journey:

> " We forthwith sailed, and in a three days' run
> We took the land; and eight and twenty days
> We crossed a desert after, where our food
> Failed, and keen hunger fell upon us all."

In answer—as Saint Patrick believed—to his prayer, a drove of swine crossed their path, on which they fed. They also found wild honey in the wood. On that same night Saint Patrick suffered from nightmare—a not unnatural result of the abundant meal of swine's flesh and honey partaken of under the circumstances recorded, but deemed by the sufferer to be a visitation of Satan, who, as " I lay sleeping, fell on me, as a mighty mass of rock might fall." But on his calling " Helias " with all his might, he saw the sun rise in the heavens, and adds:

> " I think
> 'Twas Christ my Lord who gave my cry for help,
> And sent His succour."

And then, quoting from St. Matthew's Gospel, " It is not ye that speak, but the Spirit of your Father that speaketh in you," goes on to state:

> " Whereby again
> I suffered bondage after many years,
> Continuing till this day, from that first night."

Sir Samuel Ferguson is of opinion that the " bondage " Saint Patrick " suffered " was a spiritual bondage. " It was the first occasion," he writes, "on which he had experienced what he conceived to be the presence of an indwelling coercer of his will, to obedience to whose promptings all his subsequent life was to be conformed." This explanation seems fully warranted by the context, for in no other sense could the saint be described as enduring captivity "continuing till this day from that first night." He proceeds with his narrative, covering a period of two months, and concludes this portion of his personal history with the statement:

> "On the very night
> Following the sixtieth day, the Lord me freed
> Out of their hands. . . . And so once more,
> These few years passed, I found myself at home
> Amongst the Britons, with my family."

It must also be borne in mind that the very earliest of the "Secondary Evidences" dates from nearly two centuries after Saint Patrick's death. The "Lives," as we have said, were compiled during a period which ranges from the sixth to the eleventh century. Their statements, which embody the traditions of an uncritical age, are often contradictory. The chief motive of their compilers was religious edification. A vast mass of *mirabilia*, investing the memory of the saint with powers he was far from claiming for himself, gradually grew up, obscuring the acts and the character of the central figure—a man noble from his modesty, simplicity, disinterestedness, and singleness of aim.

Still, the fact that St. Patrick received deacon's orders, and consecration as a bishop, and would naturally require study and instruction to qualify him for his work, gives probability to the statements in these Secondary Evidences. And yet there are passages in his writings that imply that he lacked these qualifications, was unlearned and ignorant, yet considered himself sent by God, though unrecognised by man. This is chiefly observable in his "Coroticus" Epistle.

> "I, Patrick—I, a sinner and unlearned,
> Here in Hibernia constituted bishop,
> Believe most surely that it is from God
> I hold commission to be that I am,
> A proselyte and pilgrim for His love,
> Here amongst savage peoples. He who knows
> All things, knows also if this be not so."

It is certain that objections to himself, and questionings as to his authority, had been made by "certain seniors" who "opposed his mission" and held his function "in small esteem." "Men much despise me," he said elsewhere, and quotes the text, "A prophet hath no honour in his own country." He does not ascribe this to malice on their part, but meekly says:

> "My wish did not commend itself to them,
> By reason, I confess, of my defect
> In learning."

All this obviously applies to "seniors," not in Gaul, but in Britain.

Still more touching is his allusion to a sin of his youth mourned and confessed by him, and, after the lapse of thirty years of his "toilsome, hard episcopate," brought up against him by those "seniors." The tone he uses is most pathetic:

> "In my grief
> And pain of mind, I to my dearest friend
> Told what I in my boyhood, in one day,
> Yea, in one hour had done: because as yet
> I had not strength; I know not, Heaven knows,
> If, at that time, I yet had fifteen years.

* * * * *

> But I rather grieve
> For him, my dearest friend ... my friend of friends,
> To whom I did confide my very soul."

This unnamed friend seems to have been the one to whom he owed his rank as bishop. The scene is still Britain—not the Continent of Europe. His friend—

> "In that debate, wherein I had not part,
> Nor moved in it, nor was I then in Britain,
> Had in my absence battled bravely for me.
> Yea, he with his own mouth had said to me,
> "Behold, thou art deemed worthy of the grade
> Of bishop," though indeed unworthy I.
> Whence comes it then, that he should afterwards,
> In presence of them all, both good and bad,
> Thus publicly degrade me, and deny
> What, unsolicited, of his own will,
> He gladly had conceded me before?
> But God is over all: of this enough."

This Ecclesiastical Council, Synod, or Conference—whatever may have been its title, seems to have had points of resemblance with the one spoken of in the Epistle to the Galatians, in which St. Paul—whose apostleship in a somewhat similar way seems to have been called in question, emphatically describes himself as "an Apostle not of man, neither by man, but by Jesus Christ, and God the Father," and adds, "When it pleased God to reveal His Son in me, that I might preach Him among the heathen; immediately I conferred not with flesh and blood." In like manner the Apostle of Ireland asserted *his* direct and divine commission:

> "Wherefore my thanks I render unto Him
> Who in all things has been my Comforter,
> That He impeded not my going forth
> Whereon I had resolved, nor stayed the work
> Which my dear God had taught me I should do."

It seems apparent that the writings of St. Patrick himself give no countenance to the legends derived from the "Lives."

The seventh, known as the "Tripartite," and dating from the 11th century, has recently been edited, with marvellous learning and rare erudition, by Whitley Stokes, Esq., D.C.L., in the Master of the Rolls series *Rerum Britannicorum Medii Alvi Scriptores*. The Irish Tripartite had previously been translated by the distinguished Irish scholar, W. M. Hennessy, Esq., M.R.I.A., and published in Miss Cusack's "Life of St. Patrick."

In this, the latest work of Dr. Whitley Stokes, he gives a summary of the legendary matter contained in these "Lives," and in especial in the fifth Life, by Probus, as follows:

"The kernel of fact in this story seems to be that Patrick returned to Ireland on, or soon after, his ordination as priest (say in A.D. 397), and without any commission from Rome; that he laboured for thirty years in converting the pagan Irish, but met with little or no success; that he attributed this failure to the want of episcopal ordination and Roman authority; that, in order to have these defects supplied, he went back to Gaul (say in A.D. 427), intending ultimately to proceed to Rome; that he spent some time in study with Germanus of Auxerre; that, hearing of the failure and death of Palladius, who had been sent on a mission to Ireland, by Pope Celestinus in A.D. 431, he was directed by Germanus to take at once the place of the deceased missionary; that Patrick thereupon relinquished his journey to Rome, received episcopal consecration from a Gaulish bishop, Matorix, and returned a second time to Ireland, about the year 432, when he was sixty years old, as a missionary from the Gaulish Church, and supplied with Gaulish assistants and funds for his mission."

The Secondary Evidences have been thus tabulated by Dr. Whitley Stokes. The late Dr. Todd, in his "St.

Patrick Apostle of Ireland," and the late Rev. J. Shearman, in his " Loca Patriciana," with other authors, came to the conclusion that there were two or more Patricks, and that the *Acta* must be assigned to more missionaries in Ireland than one. "It is plainly impossible," wrote Sir Samuel Ferguson on this topic of the Secondary Evidences, "to refer all these incidents, literally, as they stand recorded, to a single actor. The reader must either reject such of them as are too early and too late respectively, and refer the residue to the Patrick of popular belief, or else accept the alternative of allocating such of these as appear to stand on an historical basis amongst several Patricks. . . . With these aids a reasonably consistent account of the Patrick of the Secondary Evidences, in his youth, captivity, continental career, and Irish mission, might be constructed. But if this portraiture be compared with the Patrick of the Primary Evidences, a moral discrepancy, to some minds more embarrassing than any difficulty of date or person, has to be encountered. For, if the characters presented in the one set of proofs and in the other are to be reconciled, it must be by believing that a conscientious missionary, following in the track of an authorized predecessor, has arrogated to himself all the credit of what had been accomplished by Palladius, if not by Palladius and others; and that a candid student, educated in the best schools of the west of Europe, should be found lamenting not only his want of learning, but his want of the opportunities of acquiring it."

This moral difficulty remains, and is a formidable one. Is it possible to conceive that the simple, honest, earnest servant of God, and evangelizer of the Pagan Irish, whose attractive personality stands revealed in his Autobiography, could have tacidly assumed for himself the credit of other workers in the missionary field? Let the reader bear in mind that the Primary Evidences—his *scriptio sua*—are one or two hundred years earlier in date than any of the "Lives," and six centuries older than the "Tripartite" Life, and judge accordingly of their relative value as historic testimony.

It remains only to refer to the scholars in our own day who have elucidated the early Christian history of Ireland. The theme is a wide one—too wide fully to enter on here. But we may cite the honoured names of Petrie, Todd, and Shearman—no longer with us: of Reeves, Stokes, Hennessy, King, Olden, G. T. Stokes, in the paths of historic research; of Edwin, Earl of Dunraven, and Margaret Stokes, in art and architecture; while in literature D'Arcy M'Gee, D. F. M'Carthy—no longer with us—and Aubrey de Vere, happily still left to us, have found poetic inspiration in the lives of Ireland's Saints.

M. C. FERGUSON.

20 North Great George's Street, Dublin,
August, 1888.

THE PATRICIAN DOCUMENTS.

I. THE additional material recently supplied to Patrician criticism invites to a review of the evidences, as they at present stand, bearing on the principal questions which have been raised regarding the writer of the *Confessio Patricii* and the *Coroticus* Epistle; namely, as respects— (*a*) his place of origin, (*b*) his career before entering on his Irish mission, and (*c*) his epoch in time.

II. It is obvious, that in any general review of these evidences, the *Confessio* and *Coroticus*, as purporting to come from the hand of Patrick himself, ought to occupy the first place and be considered in their entirety; because whatever, in subsequent evidences, may conflict either with their general tenor, or with particular facts vouched by them, must be esteemed of less authority. As between the two documents themselves, the *Confessio*, although probably later in date, yet, as containing the record of the earlier events in the life of the writer, is given the precedence.

III. Assuming its authenticity, it is not only (next, perhaps, to the *Coroticus*) the oldest document in British history, but it affords a close and intimate view of the nature and mental disposition of one of the greatest of Christian missionaries.

IV. The texts used are those of the Book of Armagh and of Fell, 1, in the Bodleian Library, very faithful copies of which are to be found in the Appendix to Part II. of the Facsimiles of National MSS. of Ireland. The Bodleian text, as well as other exemplars used by Ware and the Bollandists, contains considerably more matter than is to be found in the older transcript in the Book of Armagh. But that transcript bears many internal evidences of abridgment; and there is nothing in the more copious matter of the other copies necessarily at variance with it, so far as it has come down to us. The translation, therefore, has been grounded on both, distinguishing those parts not found in the Book of Armagh by technical indications, but preserving the continuity of the united texts. Both texts are more or less corrupt and defective—the Bodleian one exceedingly so. In neither of them can reliance be placed on the punctuation; and the divisions of sentences and paragraphs have to be adjusted to the apparent contexture of the writer's thoughts. Most of these blemishes have, no doubt, arisen from the carelessness of copyists; but the generally ungrammatical form and inartificial sequences of the composition are due, I would suppose, to the writer's imperfect knowledge and difficult use of the Latin language, to which he himself bears repeated testimony.

V. A literal prose translation, reflecting all the discontinuances and hesitancies of the original, would indeed repel most readers from the necessary task of collecting the general sense and bearing of the whole piece, and would scarcely at all realize the intense pervading fervor and—however obstructed in its utterances—the characteristic effusiveness of the original. To convey these in English prose would require something more in the nature of a free paraphrase, which would not be an acceptable constituent in a critical essay. What appears to me a less repellent and more exact form in which to present the piece, as combining literalness with suitability for the expression of that fervent and effusive feeling which underlies its broken Latinity, is a close version in English blank verse. That even rhymed English verse may rival the closest prose in conciseness, we may see in the "Essay on Man," the "*Religio Laici,*" and other poems in our language. Blank verse, untrammelled by the necessities of rhyme, holds to the word and thought still closer. Indeed, no prose could, without affectation, admit such closeness as is allowable and congenial to this medium of translation. No translation, however, whether prose or metrical, can dispense with the very words of the original where questions of meaning are involved; but these are as easy to be cited in foot notes, in the one presentation of the general context as in the other.

VI. Translation from one language into another is often like the natural process of freezing—the product exceeding in bulk the producing material. But in English translation from Latin, this need not be so. The number of words must indeed be greater, but the whole verbal bulk may be, and in the present instance will be found to be, less. In the Latin, which expresses by inflections what we in English accomplish by the use of auxiliary particles, fewer words suffice, but these greatly exceed their English equivalents in syllabic length. Thus, in the Latin version of the Lord's Prayer there are but forty-nine words as against fifty-five in the English version; but the latter has only seventy-four syllables in its fifty-five words as against one hundred and three syllables in the forty-eight words of the former.

VII. A version from the Latin, keeping within these limits, may be accepted as possessing the closeness of literal prose; and English blank verse need not exceed them, and may yet retain enough of freedom to reflect an original conceived with loftiness and energy. The version of the *Confessio* here presented will be found to come within the limits I have indicated. I believe it contains nothing that is not found in the original, and omits nothing of any materiality that is there found. It is a long time since a communication so entirely within the department of Polite Literature has been read before the

Academy; but in the intervals of scientific and antiquarian discovery we shall not in any degree be outside our privileged pursuits, or wanting in duty to the other objects which they are designed to promote, if we occasionally addict ourselves to what our fathers have, I may be allowed to say, wisely designated the *Litteræ Humaniores*.

VIII.

THE "CONFESSIO" OF SAINT PATRICK.

[The passages ending with (A) are from the Armagh Codex; those ending with (B) are from the Bodleian.]

(Before A.D. 500).

    I, Patrick, sinner, most unlearned of all
The Faithful, and of many most despised,
Had, for my father, Deacon Calphurn, son
Of Presbyter Potitus, of a place
5 Called Bannow of Tabernia, near whereto
He owned his country dwelling; and 'twas there
I suffered capture, then not full sixteen.
    I knew not the true God; and, led away
Into captivity, with thousands more,
10 Was brought to Ireland—fate too well deserved.
For we from God had far withdrawn ourselves;
We kept not His commandments; and our priests,
Who urged salvation on us, heeded not;
And God upon us justly brought the wrath
15 Of His up-rousing, and dispersed us forth
Amongst the heathen, to the world's far end,
Here, where my Littleness may now be seen
'Mongst strangers; here, where God set free the sense
Receptive in my heart of unbelief,
20 That, even late, I should recall my sins,
And turn myself with all my heart to Him,
The Lord, who did regard my Smallness then

With pity for my youth and innocence;
Who, ere I knew Him, had me in His charge;
25 Yea, ere I knew to choose 'twixt good and ill,
Admonished me and gave me consolation,
As father might a son. And, therefore, now
I will not hide, nor could I, were it fit
To hide, such boons, such graces, as my Lord
30 Has deigned me here in my captivity.
  And this my poor return; that having attained
The touch and apprehension of my God,
I should with high exalted heart, in face
Of all that lives below all skies, confess
35 That other God nor was, nor is, nor shall be,
Save but the Lord, the Father unbegotten,
Without beginning, out of whom proceeds
Every beginning; He who in His hand
Holds all things as aforesaid; and His Son
40 Our Lord Christ Jesus, who, we do confess,
Was with the Father ere the worlds began;
Begotten of the Father spiritually,
In wise unspeakable, ere aught made was.
By Him were all things made, things visible
45 And things invisible. He was made Man,
And, conquering death, returned again to heaven.
And God gives Him all power o'er every name
Of things in earth and heaven and things in hell,
That every tongue may own that Jesus Christ
50 Is Lord and God, in whom we do believe
And wait His coming when He shall be judge
Of living and of dead; who shall repay
To each according to his deeds; and He
It is who pours on us abundantly
55 The gift and comfort of the Holy Spirit
And certain hope of immortality;

Who makes the well-believing and obedient
Sons of the Father, co-heirs with Himself,
Christ, whom we do confess and do adore,
60 One God in Trinity of holy name.
    Now He Himself has, by His prophet, said:
*Call upon Me in tribulation's day,
And I will free, and thou shalt sound My praise.*
And said again: *To show forth and confess*
65 *The works of God is very honourable.*
Therefore, though but ill-taught in many things,
I would my brethren and my friends to know
What kind I am, and that they may behold
The very thought that rises in my soul.
70 I not ignore the witness that my Lord
Doth witness by the Psalmist: *They that speak
Lies shall ye lose;* nor, yet again, *The mouth
That lies, shall lose his soul;* and our said Lord
Saith in the Gospel thus: *The idle word*
75 *Men use, for it each soul that lives shall give
Account and reckoning at the Judgment Day.*
So me with fear and trembling it behoves
To dread the doom of liars, in that same day
When none can draw aside or hide himself,
80 But all must yield account, yea, of the least
Of all their faults before the chair of Christ.
    Wherefore long time I've had in mind to write,
But up to now abstained me; for I feared
Lest I should fall in censure of men's tongues:
85 Because I have not read as others have,
Who, excellently versed in civic law*

---

* "Excellently versed in Civic law:" *Qui optime itaque jure et sacras literas utroque pari modo combiberunt*, with the annotation in margin *Incertus liber hic.*

B

And sacred letters, in a like degree,
Have never since their childhood changed their speech,
But rather made it perfecter by use;
90 Whereas this speech and utterance of mine
Is here transformed into another tongue;
And, by the savour of the style I use,
'Tis easy to be judged how I've been taught *
And trained in diction. As the Wise One saith,
95 *Sense, knowledge, and the doctrine of the truth
Show by the tongue.* But what avails excuse
Beside the fact? when here ye all may judge
The actual way in which, in my old age,
I strive at what, in youth, I never learned.
100 For then my sins obstructed. I was still,
When captured, but a lad, a beardless boy,
That knew not what to seek or what to shun.
Therefore to-day it shames me to disclose
My ignorance; because I have not learned
105 With brevity and elegance of speech
To treat deep things, as, how the Spirit moves
The soul's affections and the human mind.
But were it given me, as it is to some,
I would not long be slow to sing His praise,
110 Even though to some perchance in this I seem
Presumptuous, with my rude and stammering tongue.
Yet it is written that *the stammering tongue*
Shall yet be swift to speak the words of peace.

---

* "How I've been taught:" *Sicut facile potest probari ex aliue* [*ex salivâ*] *scripturae meae qualiter sum ego in sermonibus instructus atque eruditus*, would be nearer the drift of the original if expressed:
  "'Tis easy to be judged what kind of school
  I've been brought up in."
Sum ego = *ta me*, in the Irish.

How much the more, then, lies that charge on us
115 Who, *Christ's Epistles*, to the world's far ends
Bear word of His salvation ; not, indeed,
Learned words, but words of power *writ in our hearts,*
Not with pen-ink, but by the Spirit of God.
Yea and again that Spirit testifies
120 *Unlearning also comes from the Most High.*
Wherefore I, chief and first of the unlearned,
God's runaway, untaught, who nothing know
How to provide the morrow, surely know
This, that, before my happy humbling came,
125 I was as is a stone that, in deep mire,
Lies on the highway : and He came, who can,
And, in His pity, thence did lift me up
And set me on the wall-top. Therefore I
Will now be bold and eager-prompt to pay
130 The tribute of my praises to the Lord
Who has bestowed His everlasting boons
So great on me as pass the mind of man.
 Wherefore all ye who fear the Lord, admire,
Both great and small; and ye, ye great and learned,
135 Lords of the land, and Rhetoricians,
Hear and enquire, who was it raised me up,
Me, foolish me, from midst of them esteemed
Wise men and law-learned, and in power of speech,
As in all else, prepotent, and inspired
140 Me, even me, the butt of this world's scorn,
Above the rest, to be what now I am
Here, whilst at least with fear and reverence
Faithful in heart and uncomplainingly
I serve this people, to whom the charity
145 Of Christ assigns me, for my rest of life.
If I be worthy; that, with humble heart
And truthful lips, I teach it, in the faith

And measure of the Holy Trinity.
　　Behoves me, therefore, fearless of rebuke
150　Or danger, that I do set forth the gift
　　And everlasting consolation
　　Of God; and fearlessly declare His name
　　Abroad where'er I be: that also, so,
　　After my death, I leave, as my bequest *
155　Amongst the children of my baptism,
　　These many thousands. Not, indeed, that I
　　Was worthy that my Lord his servant poor
　　Should so far favor, after all the toils,
　　The hardships heavy, and the captive years
160　Borne 'mongst this people;—should bestow such grace
　　As, till I came to Ireland,† I nor knew
　　Nor ever hoped. But, herding daily here,
　　And often in the day saying my prayers,
　　Daily there more and more did grow in me
165　The fear of God. And holy fear and faith
　　Increased in me, that in a single day
　　I've said as many as a hundred prayers,
　　And in the night scarce fewer; so that oft
　　In woods and on the mountain I've remained,
170　And risen to prayer before daylight, through snow,
　　Through frost, through rain, and yet I took no ill,
　　Nor was there in me then aught slow as now,
　　For then the Spirit of God within me burned.
　　　And there it was, one night, in sleep, I heard
175　A voice that said to me: "Thou fastest well

---

* "Bequest:" *Ex agallias*: the word divided so between end of one line and beginning of another. *Exagalliae*—Du Cange.

† "'Till I came to Ireland:" *quod ego in iuuentute mea nunquam speraui neque cogitaui sed postquam in hiberione deueneram*: where *sed*, as in line 231, *post*, seems to be used in the sense of the Irish *acht=nisi*.

That soon shalt see thy land and home again."
Soon after which, again, I heard the voice,
And this is what it said : "Behold thy ship
Is ready," but the ship lay nowise near,
180 But nigh two hundred miles off, and where I
Had never been before, and no man knew.
So, thereupon, I turned myself to flight,
Leaving* the man whom I had served six years;
And by the help of God, who showed me well†
185 The way to go, nought dreading, found the ship.
But it, before I came, had left its place
And lay elsewhere. I craved to go on board.
My suit displeased the Master: with harsh speech
He answered me, " Thou shall not come with us."
190 Which when I heard, I left them there, to reach
My hut wherein I lodged, and as I went
Began to pray. Before my prayer was done,
I heard one of them calling after me,
" Come, for in faith we did receive thee ; come,
195 Make friendship with us in what way thou wilt."
And so, that day, I did make friends with them,
Out of God's fear, and for, besides, I hoped
To hear them yet say, " Come, in faith of Christ."
For Heathens were they. So I clave to them.
200 We forthwith sailed, and, in a three days' run,
We took the land; and eight and twenty days
We crossed a desert, after : where our food
Failed, and keen hunger fell upon us all.
Then one day, said the Master thus to me,

---

* "Leaving the man :" *intermisi hominem.* "I separated from the man," as if the thought expressed in this singular use of *intermitto* had been conceived in some form of the Irish *etar-scairim*, that is, *inter-separo*.
† "Well," *ad bonum,* as in the Irish *go maith.*

205 " What, Christian, you who say your God is great,
    Good, and Almighty, why not pray for us
    Who perish here of hunger, where the face
    Of men is hardly seen?" Then I spoke thus
    Before them all: "Turn ye your sinful hearts:
210 Convert you to the Lord my God, to whom
    Nought is impossible, that He, this day,
    Send you whereof ye yet may eat your fill;
    For all things everywhere abound with Him."
    God aiding, so it was. Behold, a drove
215 Of swine came on the road before our eyes.
    Many they slew; two nights we tarried there
    Well nourished, and our dogs filled full: for they
    Were semi-starved, and many left we there
    Half dead beside the way. Then praise to God
220 All gave, and I much honour in their sight
    Obtained, and thenceforward, abundantly
    Fared we. Wild honey also in the wood
    Found they, and offered of it, and one said,
    " 'Tis sacrificial; taste." I tasted none;
225 For which, thank God. On that same night I lay
    Sleeping, when Satan sorely troubled me,
    As well I shall remember, for as long
    As in this mortal body I shall be.
    He fell upon me, as a mighty mass
230 Of rock might fall, so that in all my limbs
    Remained not but so much* of power as brought
    Into my mind the thought to cry, "Helias."
    With which word in my mouth, I saw the sun
    Rise in the heavens; and while I cried, "Helias,"
235 With all my might. its radiance fell on me,

---

* "But so much:" *et nihil membrorum praeualens sed unde mihi uenit in spiritum ut heliam uocarem. Sed=acht=nisi*, as in page.

And banished all my torpor: and I think
'Twas Christ, my Lord, who gave my cry for help,
And sent His succour. Even so, I hope,
'Twill be hereafter, in the dreadful day
240 Of my last pressure. And the Gospel says (A),
*In that day testifies the Lord Himself,
The Spirit of the Father it is that speaks
Within you* (B), *not yourselves.* (Whereby) again
I suffered bondage,* after many years
245 Continuing till this day, from that first night.
And so remained I in their company,
But heard the same voice I had heard before
Say, "Two full months shalt thou abide with them."
And so it was: for, on the very night
250 Following the sixtieth day, the Lord me freed
Out of their hands. He gave us food and fire,
Daily dry weather too, till, at the last,
Upon the tenth day, when we all arrived,—
Days eight and twenty in the desert spent,
255 As is above said †—there remained to us

---

* "Again I suffered bondage:" *sicut in æuangelio inquit dominus non uos estis* (A), *qui loquimini sed spiritus patris uestri qui loquitur in uobis et iterum post annos* (B) *multos adhuc capturam dedi ea nocte prima* (A). A passage of great obscurity, here brought into the apparent sequence of the narrative by the introduced "whereby." The subject, too long to discuss in a note, is examined in par. xxix., *post.*

† "As is above said:" *nocte illa sexagessima liberauit me dominus de manibus eorum etiam in itinere præuidit nobis cibum et ignem et siccitatem cotidie donec* x. *decimo die peruenimus omnes sicut superius insinuaui* xx. *et* viii. *disertum iter fecimus et ea nocte qua peruenimus,* &c. To whichever antecedent the words of reference *sicut superius insinuaui* relate, it is evident that the twenty-eight days in the desert were part of one continuous journey (*post,* xxx.), commencing at the Irish shore, and ending at Patrick's home *in Brittanis.* The discrepancy in numbers is, no doubt, due to errors of transcription.

No morsel left of food; and (so), * once more,
These few years passed, I found myself at home
Amongst the Britons † with my family,
Who all received me as they might a son,
260 And earnestly besought me, that at length
After these many perils I had borne,
I never more would leave them.
                              It was there
In a night vision I beheld a man
Coming as 'twere from Ireland. Victor he.
265 Innumerable letters bore he: one
He gave to me to read. I read one line,
"The voices of the Irish," so it ran.
And while I read, methought I heard the cry
Of them that by the wood of Focluth dwell,
270 Beside the Western Ocean, saying thus,
"Come, holy youth, and walk amongst us. Come!"
All with one voice. It touched me to the heart,
And I could read no more; and so awoke—
Thank God at last who, after many years,
275 Has given to them according to their cry!
    And, on another night, I know not, I,
God knows, if 'twas within me or without,
One prayed with words exceeding exquisite
I could not understand, till, at the close,
280 He spoke in this wise—"He who gave his soul
For thee, is He who speaks." I woke with joy.
And once I saw Him—praying, as it were
Within me, and I saw myself as though

---

* "So," introduced as "whereby," above.

† "Amongst the Britons:" *in Britannis* as in the Irish gloss on Fiacc, *in bretnaib.*

THE CONFESSIO.

Within myself, and over me, that is
Over the inner man, I heard Him pray
Strongly with urgent groans, myself the while
Amazed, and wondering who should pray in me,
Till, at the very ending of his prayer,
He showed, a bishop.* I awoke and called
To memory what His apostle says—
*The Spirit helps the weakness of our prayer ;
For when we pray, and know not as we ought
What to pray for, the Spirit Himself doth pray
For us with groanings inexpressible
Not to be put in words.* And yet again,
The Lord our Advocate doth plead for us (A).
 And when † some certain of my seniors came
Against my toilsome, hard episcopate,
And made impeachment of me for my sins,
In that day truly I was tempted sore
To fall both now and everlastingly.
But the Good Lord, for His name's sake, did spare
His proselyte and pilgrim, so as I
Out of that treading-under came not ill
With stain and shame upon me. I pray God
It be not made occasion to themselves

"He showed, a bishop :" *Sic efficiatus est ut sit episcopus.* It might be conjectured to be mistranscription for *sic effatus est ut sis episcopus ;* but the internal presence of the great bishop of souls seems more consistent with the context.

† "And when :" *Et quando temptatus sum ab aliquantis senioribus meis qui venerunt . . . contra laboriosum episcopatum meum.* When ? Where ? Whence did the seniors come ? and was the episcopate prospective or subsisting ? The answers to these questions depend in great measure on the *terminus a quo* from which the thirty years, next mentioned, are to be computed.

Of sin. They found me, after thirty years,*
To charge me with one word I had confessed
Before I was a deacon. In my grief
310 And pain of mind I to my dearest friend
Told what I in my boyhood, in one day,
Yea, in one hour had done :—because as yet
I had not strength : I know not, Heaven knows,
If, at that time, I yet had fifteen years.—
315 I had not yet believed the living God
Even from my childhood; but remained in death
And unbelief till sore chastised I was
By hunger, nakedness, and enforced toil
Daily in Ireland,—for I came not here
320 Self-sent—until, indeed, I almost sank.
Yet these were rather boons to me, because,
So chastened by the Lord, I now am made
What once was far from me, that I should care
Or labour for the weal of others, I
325 Who then took no thought even for myself.
On which same day when these my elder ones
Rebuked me (B), in a vision of the night,
I saw a script against me,† and no name

---

* "After thirty years :" *Post annos triginta invenerunt me.* If the *terminus a quo* be referred to the commission of the fault, *invenerunt* must be read as in the sense of moral detection, which is difficult. If read as in the ordinary sense of finding out topically, the *terminus* should apparently be referred to Patrick's departure on this Irish mission. But see *post,* l. 419.

† "I saw a script against me :" *vidi in vissu noctis scriptum erat contra facem meam sine honore et inter haec audiui responsum dicentem male audiuimus [scripto contra] faciem designati nudato nomine.* A most difficult passage, not helped by the corresponding Bodleian text. *Contra faciem* is perhaps the Irish *in ayaid* "adversum ; " and, in that sense, the passage may be made to bear the meaning it has in the version, by introducing the two words in brackets, but otherwise seems hopelessly obscure. For *male audio,* in the sense given, see the examples in Facciolati, "*audio.*"

Of honor written, and, the while, I heard
330 That voice within make answer, "We are here
Ill-styled by name stripped bare of dignity."
It was not "Thou art here ill-styled," it said,
But "we," as if the Speaker joined himself
Incorporately with me, and the voice
335 Were His who once said, *Whoso toucheth thee,*
Toucheth as 'twere the apple of mine eye.
Wherefore my thanks I render unto Him
Who in all things hath been my comforter,
That He impeded not my going forth
340 Whereon I had resolved, nor stayed the work
Which my dear God had taught me I should do;
Nay, rather felt I as from Him new strength
Infused. And so before both God and man
My faith was proved, wherein I boldly say
345 My conscience reprehends me in no wise,
Now, nor yet will. I take to witness God
I have not lied relating what I heard
In these communings (A). But I rather grieve
For him, my dearest friend, that we should need
350 To hear such answer* given—my friend of friends
To whom I did confide my very soul—
And certain brethren had advertised me
That he, before that inhibition made,†
In that debate wherein I had not part
355 Nor moved I it, nor was I then in Britain—
Had in my absence battled bravely for me.
Yea, he with his own mouth had said to me,
"Behold, thou art deemed worthy of the grade

---

* "Hear such answer:" *Cur hoc meruimus asidire tale responsum,* referring apparently to "we are here ill-styled," *supra.*

† "Before that inhibition:" *ante defensionem illam.*

Of Bishop;" though indeed unworthy I.
360 Whence comes it, then, that he should afterwards,
In presence of them all, both good and bad,
Thus publicly degrade me, and deny
What, unsolicited, of his own will,
He gladly had conceded me before?
365 But God is over all : of this enough.
    No; I must (not) conceal* the gift of God
Which, in this land of my captivity,
He hath bestowed me, which with earnest quest
I sought for and here found. He me hath saved
370 From all unrighteousness; and I believe
By reason of the indwelling comity,
And trust in Him which, even to this day
Doth work within me audibly.† He knows
Were these man's voices. Had they been, belike
375 Christ's charity had made me hold my peace.
    Therefore unwearied thanks I render Him
Who kept me faithful in temptation's hour,
That I to-day should live to offer up
Myself a living sacrifice to Him,
380 My Saviour, my Preserver. Well may I
Say, Lord, what am I, or my calling what
That with such favor, with such aid divine
Thou hast environed and uplifted me,
As daily I amongst the Gentiles rise
385 Higher and higher, whilst I glorify
Thy name where'er I be. Whate'er befalls
Happy or wretched, good or ill, the same
I deem; and equally for it thank Thee
With thanks perpetual for that Thou hast shown

---

* " I must (not) conceal: " *Sed tamen debeo abscondere: non* omitted in text?
† " Audibly," *audi.nter.*

390 Him the most sure indubitable One,
    In whom I may believe for ever; Him
    Who will for ever hear me. So, too, I,
    In these last days, though ignorant, may dare
    Address me to a work so holy-good,
395 So wondrous, as may even make parity
    'Twixt me and them, who, He himself foretold
    Should bear His joyful message, witnessing
    Him to all people, ere the world should end.
    And we do witness here, the Gospel now
400 Is preached so far as no man is beyond (B).
    'Twere long, in whole or part, to tell my toils,
    Or how the Almighty One did oft release
    Me from enslavement; and from perils twelve,
    Wherein my life was ventured; and from snares,
405 The which I cannot put in words. 'Twere ill
    Too much to tax my reader where I have
    The Author's self within, who all things knows,
    Even before they happen, as He knows
    Me, his poor pupil. And for that it is
410 The voice divine doth oft admonish me :
    Whence came this wisdom to me who had none,
    Nor knew the number of my days nor Him?
    Whence came this knowledge and this heart's delight
    In this His gift so great, so salutary,
415 That, for its sake, I well contented left
    Country and kin? And many were the gifts
    They offered me with yearning and with tears.
    And certain of my seniors, too, made known
    Their disapproval;* but with the help of God

---

* "Their disapproval." If this be the same opposition of the seniors above related (l. 297), and again in more general terms referred to, *post* (l. 556-60), it should be deemed to have preceded Patrick's mission, whatever difficulty that construction might entail in interpreting *invenerunt*.

420 In no way did I yield them my consent :—
Not mine the grace ; but God it was in me,
Who conquered through me and withstood them all,
That I might come to preach His Gospel here
To the Hibernian people, that I here
425 Should suffer the contempts of unbelievers
Should hear derision of my embassage,
And many persecutions, even to chains,
Endure ; nay, even my own patrician grade
Forfeit for others' good. And if I be
430 But worthy to do somewhat for His name,
Ready I am, this hour, with all my heart,
To yield Him service, even to my death,
Who this grace does me that, through means of me,
Much people is re-born to God, confirmed,
435 And clerks ordained for their instruction,
New coming to the faith from earth's far ends,
And gathered to the Lord, even as, of old,
He promised by His prophet, *They shall come
From outmost ends of earth ;* and also says,
440 *Our fathers got them idols, and therein
Had nothing profitable ;* and again
This also : *I have set thee as a light
To light the Gentile, that thou shouldst make safe
Even to the ends of earth.* And here I wait
445 To see fulfilled His words, who ne'er deceived,
As promised in the Gospel,—*They shall come
From east and west, and sit down side by side
With Abraham and with Isaac and with Jacob.*
Even so do we believe from all the world
450 The faithful come. Behoves it, therefore, we
Fish well and diligently, as the Spirit says,
*Come after Me that I may make of you
Fishers of men ;* and, by His prophet, again,

Behold, of fishermen and hunters keen
455 *I send a multitude; so saith the Lord.*
Et cætera.* Whereby it much behoves
We spread our nets in such wise as a shoal
And multitude be taken; and that clerks
Be everywhere at hand who may baptize
460 The hastening crowd, even as our good Lord saith
In His evangel, *Going, therefore, forth,*
Teach ye all nations, and the same baptize
In name of Father, Son, and Holy Ghost,
Teaching them to observe what things soe'er
465 *I have commanded; and, lo, I myself*
Am with you till the final consummation
Of all things; and again says, *Going forth*
Into the whole world, preach ye my evangel
To every creature living. Who believes
470 *And is baptized, is safe. Who not believes,*
He shall be damned † (A). And He again says thus:
The gospel of my kingdom shall be preached
To the whole world; and witness shall be made
To all the nations, and then comes the end.
475 Likewise our Lord doth by His prophet say,
Lo, in the latter days, thus saith the Lord,
I shall pour forth my Spirit on all flesh.
Your sons and daughters they shall prophesy,
Your youths see visions, and old men dream dreams.
480 *And on your servants and your handmaidens*

---

* "*Et cætera:*" Probably an indication of abridgment (iv. *supra*).
† The words "reliqua sunt exempla" here occur in the Armagh Codex, left untranslated, as being probably the language of the scribe, indicating abridgment from a fuller text.

*In these days shall I pour my Spirit, and they
Shall prophesy.* And also Hosee says,
*Her will I call my people who was not
My people, and on her will pity take*
485 *On whom I took not pity; and in the place
Wherein 'twas said no people of mine are ye,
There shall they yet be called the sons of God* (B).
    Whence now the Irish, who, in former days,
Had but their idols and their rites unclean,
490 Nor aught knew of the Lord, have late become
The Lord's own people. And the sons of Scots
And daughters of their kings, now sons of God
Are counted, and vowed handmaidens of Christ (A).
And one bless'd Scotic lady nobly born,
495 A most fair person whom myself baptized,
Came, soon thereafter, making her report
Of intimation by a messenger
Sent her from God with His admonishment
That virgin she should live and nearer Him.
500 In six days after,—thank the Lord for it,—
With excellent observance she assumed
The grade desired of all Christ's handmaidens:
Not at their parents' bidding. They from them
Suffer reproach and persecution,
505 Yet, notwithstanding, still the number grows
Of those of our kind daily born to us
I know not, I, how many they are, besides
Widows and women continent; of whom
They chiefly suffer who, in bondage held,
510 Bear threats and terrors: yet they persevere,
And God to many of them grants the grace
That, if but in a little, earnestly
They follow His example. Whence it comes
Should I now care to leave them, going forth

515 It may be into Britain,* sure 'twere sweet
To see one's country and one's kin again :
Or farther yet proceeding, even to Gaul,
To see the brethren, and the faces see
Of my Lord's saints, God knows I were right glad,
520 But in the Spirit am bound : and He declares
I were God's recreant did I leave them so.
Moreover, truth it is, I would not lose
The fruit of all my labour well begun.
Yet 'tis not I determine, but my Lord,
525 He who commanded I should hither come,
That here I should fulfil my rest of days
In serving them : and so methinks I shall :
Albeit but little trust I in myself,
Clad in this body of death, for he is strong
530 Who daily struggles to subvert my faith,
And turn me from the unfeigned chastity
I'll keep, God helping, till my days do end.
The flesh indeed still draws us down to death,
And snares of lawless pleasure ; and I know
535 In part the reason why I cannot live
The perfect life His other faithful souls
Achieve ; but to my good Lord I avow
I blush not at His searching of my heart ;
For since I first did know Him in my youth,
540 His love and fear have ever grown in me,
And I, He helping, still have kept the faith.
Let him who will, then, laugh : let him who will,
Scoff. I shall not keep silence, nor conceal

---

* "Going forth, it may be into Britain, &c. :" *ut pergens in britanniis et libentissime paratus eram quasi ad patriam et parentes non id solum sed usque gallias usitare fratres et ut uiderem faciem sanctorum domini mei.* In some of the MSS. the words are *fratres meos.*

The signs and marvels ministered to me
545 Of God, who knoweth all things many years
Before they are; yea, from before all time.
Wherefore ought I unintermittingly
Give thanks to Him that He did so indulge
My ignorance and sloth, not once but oft;
550 And not as with an object of just wrath
Dealt with me, but as with His yoke-fellow,
Though slow I was to learn the part enjoined,
And by the Spirit shown; who pitied me
'Mongst thousand thousands other; for He saw
555 That I was wil'ing-ready, but knew not
In what way to bear witness: for they all*
Opposed my mission, and, behind my back,
Did prate and say, "This one, forsooth, would put
His life in jeopardy 'mongst enemies,
560 Who of the Lord know nothing," not as though
They spoke in malice: but, indeed, because
My wish did not commend itself to them,
By reason, I confess, of my defect
In learning. And I did not recognise
565 At once the grace that then was in me—grace
Now efficacious as it then had been,
Had I been as I ought.
      Thus simply, then,
Brethren and fellow servants in the Lord
Who have believed with me, I've told to you
570 How it has come to pass that, for the sake
Of strengthening and confirming you in faith,
I have preached, and still do, hoping we all
May yet rise higher. That be my reward!
Because *the wise son is his father's glory.*

---

* "They all:" See *ante* l. 419.

575 You know, and God knows, what way from my youth
    I have conversed amongst you, in the faith
    Of truthfulness and singleness of heart:
    That to the people I do dwell amongst
    I have declared the faith, and so do still.
580 God knows that I no man of them in aught
    Have circumvened, nor, for the sake of Him
    And of His Church, will ever; nor provoke
    In them, or anyone, uncharity,
    Whereby the name of God may be blasphemed
585 In me, for it is written, *Wo to him
    By whom the name of God shall be blasphemed.*
    And, unlearned though I be in skill of words,
    Yet have I striven in some poor sort to serve
    My Christian brethren and Christ's handmaidens,
590 And pious women who of their free will
    Did oft bestow me gifts, and on mine altar
    Cast of their jewels, which I still returned,
    Though thereby they were grieved: and, for the hope
    Of life eternal, have so led my life,
595 Here with them, so on guard, as none may find
    In any tittle of my ministry
    Cause of offence, nor let my smallest act
    Afford occasion to the infidel
    To sully or diminish my good fame.
600   Think ye, where I such thousands have baptized,
    I took from any of them, in recompense,
    But half a scruple. Tell me when, or where?
    I will return it. Yea, where God ordained
    Through my weak ministry these many Clerks,
605 *Gratis* I gave them orders. If I asked
    Of any to the value but of my shoe,
    Tell me: I will repay it you and more.
    'Twas rather I who spent my worldly wealth

On you, amongst you, wheresoe'er I went,
610 In your behalf, through perils manifold,
So far as no man was beyond, nor there
Had ever come who might give baptism,
Ordain a clergy, or confirm the flock.
God aiding, I did, with most willing mind
615 And diligent affection to your weal,
Defray it all. Sometimes I fee'd the kings,
In that I fee'd their sons who gave convoy
To guard us all from capture. In one day
They sought, indeed, to slay me; but my time
620 Was not yet come. But all the goods they found
Upon us they bore off, and me myself
Kept bound with iron, till, the fourteenth day,
The Lord did lose me from their power; and all
Our goods were given us back, for the Lord's sake,
625 And sake of our conductors. You yourselves
Have knowledge what gratuities I spent
On them that did administer the law
Throughout the regions I most visited.
I think not less than fee of fifteen men
630 I did disburse amongst them, all, that you
Might me enjoy, and I again in you
Have manifold enjoyment in the Lord.
Nor grudge I it, nor count it yet enough.
Lo, I still spend, and still will further spend,
635 Happy if He, who can, shall yet allow
That for your sakes I even may spend my soul (B).
I call to witness God I do not lie,
Nor write as seeking opportunity
Of lucre or of flattery or reward
640 Of praise. That honour is enough for me
Which is not seen, but in the heart believed (A).
But He who promised never lies (B). I see

THE CONFESSIO.

    Myself, in this my generation,
    Beyond degree exalted by my Lord,
645 Unworthy though I am, nor such as He
    Might deign so favour. For I surely know
    That poverty and plainness fit me more
    Than luxury and riches. Christ our Lord
    Was also poor for us. I poorer still,
650 For, should I crave for wealth, I have it not.
    Nor judge I now myself: for daily now
    I look to find my death by violence,
    Or, captive, to be sold to slavery,
    Or some such end: (A) but none of these I fear,
655 Having assurance of His promises,
    For I have cast me in the hands of God
    Who governs all things, and his prophet saith,
    Cast thou thy burden on the Lord, and He
    Will aid thee. Yes, I do commend my soul
660 To my most faithful God whose embassage
    I here discharge, howe'er unworthily.
    For He respects not persons, but did choose
    Me to this office, that, amongst the crowd
    Of His ambassadors, I might be least.
665 What shall I render back to Him for all
    His benefits conferred on me? What say
    Or promise to Him when I plainly see
    I nothing have unless He gives it me,
    Yea, though I search the heart and reins. Enough,
670 More than enough I count it, well content,
    If He but give me that I drink His cup
    As granted other claimants of His love;
    But never, never let me lose the flock
    He pastures by me in earth's outland here!
675 God grant me that! And that I persevere
    In faithful witness to my journey's end.
    And if, for His sake, I have ought of good

Accomplished, for His love, I pray Him grant
That with His captives and His proselytes,
680 Even for His name's sake I may shed my blood,
Be it without my dues of burial,
Yea, though this wretched body and these limbs
Be torn asunder by devouring dogs,
Wild beasts, or fowls of heaven. I surely know
685 Did this befall me, I should so enrich
My soul with my poor body; and I know
Clad in our bodies we shall all arise
In that day, in the brightness of the sun,
To wit, in glory of Lord Jesus Christ,
690 Our dear Redeemer, rise as sons of God,
And co-heirs with Himself, conformable
To His own image as it then shall be.
 For this sun, which we see, doth daily rise
At God's commandment; but God so ordains
695 It shall not always rise, nor shall its light
Endure for ever. It shall fade, and they
That worship it shall perish: but, for us
We do believe and worship the true Sun,
Christ, which shall never perish, nor shall He
700 Who doth His will, but shall endure for ever,
As Christ Himself, who, in the heaven of heavens,
Reigns with the Father and the Holy Ghost
Now and for everlastingly—Amen.
 Again and yet again I iterate
705 My brief words of Confession, and declare
In truth, and in uplifting of the heart,
Before my God and His most holy angels,
That other object never did I look to
In coming back* again amongst this people,

---

* " In coming back : " *Ut unquam redderem [redirem] agentem [ad gentem] illam; Unde autem prius uix euaseram.* A good example of the corrupt state of the Bodleian text.

710   From whom so hardly I escaped before,
      Save but the Evangel and His promises (B).
      And now beseech all them that do believe
      And fear the Lord, whoe'er they be shall deign
      Look on this writing or receive the same
715   Which sinner Patrick, I, the much-unlearned,
      Have writ in Ireland, that no man may say
      My Ignorance it was dictated aught,
      If any aught of good be therein seen
      Such as may pleasure God, but rather deem
720   For certain that it doth proceed from Him.
      And this is my Confession e'er I die (A).

IX. The first impression made by this narrative as regards Patrick's place of origin, certainly is, that Bannow Taberniæ was in insular Britain; because in speaking of his desire to revisit his family from Ireland (viii. 518-24), he puts Gaul beyond them. The first impression also is that no great length of time elapsed between his Call and his proceeding on his mission; and that the intermediate time was spent in Britain; because he thanks God for not having impeded him in going forth (*ib.* 340) on his mission to the Irish (*ib.* 422), notwithstanding the opposition of his family and seniors, which struggle, commencing in Britain, appears to have been continuous and presumably carried on in one place. The only intimation of epoch is, vaguely, that it was in Christian times, and while a well-settled Church-organization existed in that part of Britain in which his family were settled.

X. Besides these probable matters of fact, and the lively traits of Patrick's personal character which it furnishes, the *Confessio* intimates that on some occasion—the place of which is not distinctly specified—he had experienced an injurious opposition against his "laborious episcopate," then seemingly in course of prosecution, when some personal title of distinction was withheld from him in what may be inferred to have been an ecclesiastical script (viii. 279-44), and that at some previous time, he not then being in Britain, his conduct, apparently in reference to episcopal functions, had been the subject of discussion in some assemblage, probably synodical, in that country (*ib.* 348-50).

XI. The *Coroticus* Epistle is not found with the *Confessio* in the Book of Armagh; but while the *Confessio* has always been referred to as "Epistolarum Patricii Liber Primus," the *Coroticus* has in like manner been known as "Epistolarum Patricii Liber Secundus," and, in the Book of Armagh, the entitlement under which the *Confessio* is found is "Incipiunt Libri Sancti Patricii Episcopi," showing that at least another was intended to accompany it. The *Coroticus*, as will be seen, contains much internal evidence of having proceeded from the same hand as the *Confessio* (conf. viii. 454-5, with xii. 122-4; and viii. 492-4, with xii. 134-6, &c.). It also, like the *Confessio*, uses some expressions not consonant to the Latin but to the Celtic idiom, as though the writer in both conceived his thoughts in some form of Celtic speech and expressed them in

Latin (viii. 93 *n*, 161 *n*, 183 *n*, 184 *n*, 231 *n*, 258 *n*, 328 *n*, and xii. 69 *n*, 140 *n*, 188 *n*). It is a shorter piece than the *Confessio* and in some respects less interesting. In the *Confessio* the inner nature of the writer is seen throughout. In the *Coroticus* he is seen in his relations with an external world of wrong and suffering, against which he struggles with the grief and indignation any pastor might experience whose flock had been made the prey of lawless violence. Still there breathes through its reproaches and words of technical objurgation a lofty sentiment and energy of imagination which would make any prose translation inadequate to its full reproduction. It is therefore presented here as, in form as well as substance, a companion piece to the *Confessio*. No important difference of meaning arises on any verbal discrepancy of the texts. That used by the Bollandists is here adopted, from Villanueva, who has appended notes of the various readings (*S. Patricii Synodi et opuscula*, 240).

XII.

THE "COROTICUS" EPISTLE.

(Before A.D. 500.)

    I, Patrick—I, a sinner and unlearned,
Here in Hibernia constituted bishop,
Believe most surely that it is from God
I hold commission to be that I am,
5 A proselyte and pilgrim, for His love,
Here amongst savage peoples. He who knows
All things, knows also if this be not so.
    I would not aught so harsh and so severe
From me proceeded; but constrained I am
10 By zeal for God and for the truth of Christ,
And stirred to anger for my people's sake,
My sons in God, for whom I made exchange
Of kin and country, and did vow myself
For rest of life, if worthy, even to death,
15 To teach the Heathen; though, indeed, by some
My function now be held in small esteem.
    Therefore these words I, with my proper hand,
Have framed and written, for delivery
To these the soldiers' of Coroticus;
20 I say not, to my fellow-citizens,
Nor fellow-citizens of pious Romans,
But rather fellow-citizens of Fiends,
Because of their ill deeds, who, barbarously,
In manner full of hatred, live in death,

25 Companions of the Scots and Picts apostate,
   Intent to glut their savage souls in blood
   Of innocents unnumbered, by myself
   In God begotten and in Christ confirmed.
      The day wherein my white-robed neophytes—
30 The chrism still wet and glistening on their brows-
   Passed at the sword's edge of these murderers,
   The day next following, sent I my Epistles
   By one whom from his youth I had brought up,
   A holy Presbyter, with other clerks,
35 Beseeching that some portion of their spoils
   They might forgive us, and set free again
   The baptized captives whom they still detained:
   They answered my request with jeers and laughter.
   Alas, I know not which the more to mourn,
40 Them slain, or them made prisoners, or them
   Whom Satan therein made his instruments;
   Who, with himself, must in the pains of hell
   Hereafter have their lasting recompense:
   For, *He who sins the servant is of sin,*
45 And worthy to be called the Son of Satan.
      Know ye then, all men having fear of God,
   That alien unto me and unto Him
   Whose office here I execute, are they
   Fratricides, parricides, devouring wolves
50 Who swallow up the people of the Lord
   As 'twere a meal of bread. But it is written,
   The wicked have made void Thy law. That law,
   Which in Hibernia in those latter days,
   Thou didst set up so fair and excellent.
55   God granting, I intrude on no man's right,
   But have my part, with others He has called
   And pre-appointed, to proclaim His gospel,
   Through no small persecutions, to earth's ends;

Albeit the enemy doth strive against me
60 By tyranny of this Coroticus,
Who knows not fear of God or of God's priests,
His chosen ones, to whom He delegates
The power supreme and awful: *Whatsoe'er
Ye bind on earth it shall be bound in heaven.*
65   Wherefore, beseech you, all that holy are,
And all of humble heart, that with such men
Ye hold no flattering converse. You, with them,
Eat not nor drink; nor of them take their alms,
Until with rigorous* penance, and with tears
70 Effused, they make atonement, and set free
These new-baptized handmaidens of Christ,
For whom He died and suffered on the cross.
For the Most High doth not respect the gifts
The unjust offer. *He who offers up*
75 *Out of the poor man's substance, is as he*
Who slays the son in presence of the father.
Again: *The riches he is gorged withal*
Forth from his belly he shall vomit up.
Death's messenger shall hale him, and *the ire*
80 *Of dragons shall assail him. Tongue of asp*
Shall slay him. Inextinguishable fire
Consume him. Woe to them that fill themselves
With that not theirs. What profits it a man
To gain the whole world, if he lose himself,
85 *And suffer condemnation of his soul?*
   Long were the list, to run through all the law
Denounced by God against cupidity.
Greed is a mortal sin. Thou shalt not covet
Thy neighbour's goods. Thou shalt commit no murder.

---

* "With rigorous penance:" *Crudeliter,* agreeable to the Irish *cruaid* "hard."

90 *The homicide cannot be one with Christ.*
Who hates his brother shall a murderer
Be deemed, and he who loves not his own brother
Remains in death. How much more guilty he
Who stains his hands in blood of God's own children,
95 Lately acquired to Him in earth's far ends,
Here through my Littleness's ministry. .
What! was it then without God's promises
Or in the body only that I came
To Ireland? Who compelled me? Who me bound
100 In spirit that I should no more behold
Kindred or early friend? Whence came the sense
Inspiring me with pity for the race
That once were my own captors? I was born
Noble; my father a *Decurio;*
105 That privilege of birth I have exchanged
(I blush not for it, and I grudge it not)
For benefit of others, bartered so
In Christ, and given over to a race
Extern to mine, all for the glorious hope
110 Ineffable, of that perennial life
Which is in Jesus Christ our Lord; albeit
My own not know me. And 'tis also said,
A prophet in his own land hath no honor.
Belike they think we are not of one Father
115 Nor of one sheep-fold. But the Lord declares
Who is not with me is against me. He
Who with me gathereth not, scattereth.
Ill fares it when one builds and one casts down.
And seek I not the things that are mine own?
120 Not for mine own delight: 'twas God that stirred
That strong solicitude within my heart,
That, of the hunters and the fishermen
Whom He aforetime for these latter days

Had pre-appointed, I too should be one.
125 Men bear me envy: Lord what shall I do?
Men much despise me: Lord, behold thy sheep
Are torn around me, and are made a prey
Of these aforesaid robbers, by command
Of this, Thy foe, Coroticus, whose mind
130 Is far from charity: who, Christian men
Delivers into hands of Scots and Picts.
Lord, ravening wolves have eaten up thy flock
Which here in Ireland had such fair increase,
Sons of the Scots and daughters of the Kings
135 Now holy monks and handmaidens of Christ,
So many, past my counting. Wherefore thou,
Coroticus, no pleasure in these wrongs
Done to the just hast now, nor ever shalt have,
Now nor till judgment, and the final day
140 Of condemnation to the under world.*
What man of holy life would not abhor
To jest, to feast, with such as these? They fill
Their houses with the spoils of Christians slain.
They live on rapine. Pity they know not.
145 They drink of poison; and the poisoned cup
They offer to their kindred, even as Eve
Knew not 'twas death she offered Adam. So
Fares it with all the wicked; endless death
And endless pain the fruit of all they do.
150 This custom do the Gaulish Christians use
And Roman. Fit and holy Presbyters
They send the Franks and other extern Heathens,

---

* "Of condemnation to the under-world:" *Quam obrem injuriam justorum non te placeat, etiam usque ad inferos non placebit.* "Ad inferos," equivalent to the Irish use of "go brath," to the condemnatory judgment, for ever.

With money charged, so many thousand coins,
Wherewith to ransom their baptized slaves:
155 *Thou slayest and sellest into extern lands
Which know not God, my Christians, and dost cast
Christ's baptized virgin members in a stews.*
What hope canst thou, so acting, have in God?
   Him who thinks with thee, him who to thy crime
160 Gives words approving, God will judge. For me,
I know not how to speak or what words use
Of these dead dear ones of God's family
Thy sword has touched, alas, too close. 'Tis writ,
To weep with them that weep. And writ again,
165 *If ails one member all do ail with it.*
And still the Church bewailing must lament
Those sons and daughters whom as yet the sword
Leaves living, but who live in exile far
Across the sea, where, that the sin may show
170 Fouler by want of shame, the impudent
Sits shameless and abounds; where free-born men
And Christians, sold for money, serve as slaves
To basest, wickedest, apostate Picts.
   Therefore with lamentation unrestrained
175 I will uplift my voice; oh dearest brothers,
Loveliest and most beloved, my sons in Christ
Begotten of me, past my power to count,
What shall I do for you, unworthy I,
To succour God or man? *The iniquity*
180 *Of the unjust has overcome us.* They,
Belike, believe not that one baptism
We both have been baptized in; that one God
We both have over us. Belike, think scorn
Of us, that haply Ireland gave us birth.
185 For this do I bewail you, oh my brothers.
Yet, on the other hand, do, in myself,

Rejoice that my poor toils in your behoof
And pilgrim labours were not all in vain,*
Though such unspeakable and horrid crime
190 Has happened during this my ministry.
Thank God, the baptized of you, and believing
Are gone from this place into Paradise.
I see you as ye take your parting flight
To where shall be no night nor any grief,
195 Nor ever death may enter; in whose fields,
Even as young calves let loose, ye shall exult,
And under foot tread down your enemies,
Who dust and ashes 'neath your feet shall lie.
There, with apostles and with prophets, ye
200 Shall reign, and martyrs, and eternal crowns
Enjoy; as He has witnessed, saying thus:
Coming from east and west they shall sit down
With Abraham and Isaac and with Jacob
In *kingdom of the Heavens. Without are dogs,*
205 *Sorcerers, and murderers, and perjurers,*
Whose portion shall be henceforth in the lake
Of ever-burning fire. And not in vain
The apostle tells us: *Where the justest man*
Is hardly safe, where shall the sinner look—
210 *The impious, and transgressor of the Law—*
To find himself? Where shall Coroticus,
With his most wicked rebels against Christ,
Look to be found? Where find them they who now
Bestow the baptized women and the spoils
215 Of orphans on their filthy satellites,
For sake of this world's fleeting sovereignty,
Which, in a moment, passes as a cloud,

---

* "In vain:" *in vacuum;* agreeable to the Irish idiom, *do l ar nemnid.*

Or smoke that dissipates before the wind.
So shall the sinner and the fraudulent
220 Perish before God's face. But they, the just,
Shall banquet in the heaven of heavens with Christ,
Judging the nations, and o'er unjust kings
Rule throughout ages without end. Amen.
    Before my God and His most holy angels
225 I bear my witness that it shall be so,
Even as my poor Ignorance has said it.
For these are not my words. These are the words
Of God and His apostles and His prophets,
Who never lied, which I here put in Latin.
230 *They who believe are safe. Who not believe*
They shall be damned. The voice that speaks is God's.
    I now beseech His servant, whosoe'er
Shall set him forth to be the carrier
Of these my letters, that he suffer none
235 Abstract them privily, but have them read
Before all peoples publicly, yea, read
In presence of Coroticus himself.
    May God inspire them that they think at length
Of Him, and even late although it be,
240 Repent them of the wickedness they've done.
Manslayers of their brethren in the Lord
They have been. May they yet repent, and free
Their captive baptized women; so that yet
They may themselves deserve to live in God,
245 And have eternal safety. Now be peace
To Father, Son and Holy Ghost. Amen.

XIII. This document advances us no further in the inquiry as to Patrick's place of origin than by its suggestion (xii. 19-25), that the ruler of that district, wherever situate, was Coroticus (*post*, xxxii.), and that Coroticus's soldiers, professing Christians, were Roman citizens of Patrick's own municipality there, and associates of the Picts and Scots, an indication pointing to some part of Northern insular Britain. Its contribution to Patrick's personal history is also scanty. In it (*ib.* 2) he alleges himself to be constituted bishop in Ireland; and the Epistle, denouncing the minor excommunication, is in itself an act of episcopal jurisdiction. In the exercise of his functions he intrudes on no other man's right (*ib.* 55-8), while he intimates (*ib.* 97-101) that his mission was undertaken under Divine compulsion, and that, since going forth on it, he had never again beheld the faces of his family or friends. On the question of epoch the *Coroticus* furnishes ground for wider speculation. The reference to "Apostate" Picts (*ib.* 25, 173) will, *prima facie*, strike most readers as indicating a date subsequent to the conversion of the Southern Picts by Ninian of Whiterne, about A.D. 412, the conversion of the Northern Picts by Columba in the sixth century being clearly too late, and any earlier Christianization of Scotland, rightly or wrongly, discredited. It is certain, however, that monuments of an earlier date than either Ninian or Columba, laying claim to a Christian origin, exist in Pictland, and it will be well not to allow the possibility of there having been apostate Picts before the mission of Ninian in North

THE COROTICUS EPISTLE.

Britain to be excluded from our consideration; especially as the context of the Epistle is not to be reconciled without difficulty to a post-Ninianite epoch. For, certainly, municipal institutions and the presence of a Christian Roman soldiery (*ib.* 20-1) are features more likely to be found in Northern Britain before the withdrawal of the legions and general flight of the Romans in the early part of the fifth century. To the same effect is the passage in which, reproaching Coroticus with selling fellow Christians into slavery, Patrick contrasts his conduct with that of the Christians of Gaul and Rome (*ib.* 150-56) who bestowed their treasures in redeeming baptized captives from the Franks and outside Gentiles. The meaning appears to include the Franks among the other "exteras gentes," which would look to a period prior to their removal from the right bank of the Rhine and settlement in Belgic Gaul about A.D. 428, and indeed prior to the disruption of the Romano-Gaulish civilization, by the great inroad of the barbarians about A.D. 407.

XIV. The mission of Palladius, Archdeacon of Auxerre, as first bishop to the Irish Christians by Pope Celestine in A.D. 431, rests on the cotemporaneous authority of Prosper of Aquitaine, and has never been denied or doubted. If the writer of the *Confessio* and *Coroticus* succeeded him, these Epistles penned after probably thirty years from his arrival (viii. 98, xii. 33-4), would belong to the latter part of the fifth century, and all the last-mentioned inferences as to epoch, however probably flowing from them, should be set aside. Before determining on that alternative, it will be well to enter on an examination of the other evidences.

XV. These Secondary Evidences consist of the seven Lives published by Colgan in his *Trias Thaumaturga*, and of the Collections in the Book of Armagh not accessible to him, supplemented by the valuable matter lately restored to them from the Royal Library of Brussels by the Rev. Edward Hogan in his "Documenta de S^{co}. Patricio" (*post*, xxvi.). There are other Lives in Irish Manuscripts, but they do not appear to add anything pertinent to this inquiry.

XVI. In marshalling the Lives, Colgan has given the first place to the Irish Hymn or metrical legend ascribed to Patrick's cotemporary, Fiacc, bishop of Sletty. In the arrangement of the others he has been influenced by this consideration, that he finds in them expressions to the effect that such a one "is" or "inhabits" in such a church, being a person of known date in history. Consequently, he takes these Lives to have been compiled while the persons in question were still living. But this is now recognised as a misapprehension of the expression "is," which in Irish hagiography means no more than that the relics of such a one are there preserved, or his memory there venerated. For example, in the second of Colgan's Lives the expression is used regarding Bishop Loarne of Bright in the county of Down: "Civitatula est quæ dicitur *Imreathan*, ubi est Episcopus *Loarne* qui ausus est increpare Patricium tenentem manum pueri ludentis juxta ecclesiam suam" (Vit. II.[a] c. xxxvii.). The story, as more fully told in the Vita. IV.[a] c. xxxvii., shows the idea of the kind of presence after death, thought, in these times, to be continued in the persons of buried saints. The boy's hoop with which he had been playing near the grave of Saint Patrick (Bright is not far from Saul, where the incident seems to have happened) had fallen down through a chink into the interior of the grave, The boy, having put in his hand to recover his plaything, was unable to withdraw it; on which bishop Loarne, being sent for, attended, and addressed these words to Patrick: "Cur, senior, manum innocentis tenes?"

XVII. This kind of indication affording no criterion, it will now be inquired whether Colgan's arrangement may not be supported on some other ground. One group, comprising the three last Lives, Five, Six, Seven, is easily separable as bearing internal evidence of times later than the ninth century. There remain Lives One, Two, Three, and Four, to which may be added the Collections in the Book of Armagh as now supplemented by the matter brought to light at Brussels. These Collections refer themselves to certain dates in the seventh century. Tirechan, the author of one set of them, states that he took his matter from the oral instruction or from the book of his teacher, Bishop Ultan of Ardbraccan, who died A.D. 656. Muirchu Maccu Machthine, the author of the imperfect Life constituting another part, professes to write at the dictation or by the command of his patron, Bishop Aed of Sletty, who died A.D. 698. Both profess to ground their relations on already existing material written and traditionary. Muirchu, in a preface to his work, intimates that many had already endeavoured to compile the *Acta* of Patrick, and that there was at least one "Life" of the saint then in existence; but in excusing his own imperfect style, seems to claim the merit of originality in his composition. Tirechan, in addition to the book of Bishop Ultan, refers also to a "Commemoratio" or personal memoir which he ascribes to Patrick himself.

XVIII. These circumstances invest the Patrician Collections in the Book of Armagh with distinctive importance, and, in the absence of date-indications from the other pieces, give them the character of a standard by comparison with which the relative priorities of all may be approximately estimated. This may be done in a manner sufficiently discriminative for the purposes of the present inquiry, by the application of some principles grounded on common experience. It may be laid down as matter generally observed in compositions of this kind.

First. That as between a shorter and a longer biography of the same person, the longer may be presumed to be the more recent; which presumption, in biographies of saints, is strengthened where the disparity is caused by the introduction of additional *Mirabilia*.

Secondly. That when the same matter *verbatim* is found in several pieces on the same subject, continuously in one, but discontinuously and with interspersed matter, *ejusdem generis*, in others, there is a presumption that the latter is copied from the former; especially where the author of the continuous matter claims originality for his composition, and where faults or obscurities of expression in the professing original are found corrected or avoided in the duplicate.

XIX. A careful examination of the Lives Two, Three, and Four, shows that, while each in length greatly exceeds the *Muirchu*, this excess is in a large degree made up of *Mirabilia;* that almost the whole text of *Muirchu*, in many instances chapter for chapter and word for word, interspersed with cognate matter which a copyist would not be likely to omit, exists in these Lives respectively; and that, in them, defects and obscurities of expression of *Muirchu* are rectified or avoided. For these reasons the "Colgan," Lives Two, Three, and Four, will be regarded as *puisne* in date of composition and authority to *Muirchu* as it to *Tirechan*, subject however to this reservation, that their sources may be of an equal or greater antiquity.

XX. But the Hymn of Fiacc does not afford any presumption of the same kind. It nowhere borrows the language of the other Lives. They add to and improve on the matter found in it. It gives one alias to Patrick, *Succat*. They add *Cothraige* and *Magonius*. It represents Patrick as obtaining, in compensation for not being buried, as he wished, at Armagh, two special privileges, namely, that his favourite Hymn should be a *lorica* for those who should sing it, and that, at the Last Day, all the Irish should go up with him to Judgment. To this the Lives add two further prerogatives; and the *Muirchu* improves on that respecting the Last Day by making Patrick himself the Judge of the Irish on that occasion.

XXI. A probable priority among these Secondary Evidences may therefore be assigned to the *Fiacc* already put first in his series by Colgan. In the midst of much that is vague and trivial it contains apparently the germs from which most of what has since been affirmed respecting Patrick's epoch, contemporaries, and personal history immediately before his arrival as a missionary in Ireland, appears to have grown up. In point of literary interest it is bald and jejune, like most bardic works of its class. We experience, indeed, a great change in leaving the natural effusions of Patrick himself for the vague and evasive generalities of his commemorator. The piece is in Irish, a very archaic example of the language, and is composed in rhymed verse. The necessities of the rythm lead to the employment of *chevilles* or phrases thrown in as metrical make-weights; but some of these, such "as histories relate," "as lines tell us," indicate that written material then existed, and that the writer did not, as Colgan was inclined to believe, relate cotemporaneous events. Indeed nothing in literary criticism can be clearer than that this piece was written some considerable time after the desertion of Tara, an event twice referred to in it (xxii. 10, 22), which took place about A.D. 565. It may, if I have given it its proper priority, have been composed at any time during the period which elapsed after Tara had become "desert and silent," and before the middle of the seventh century, when Tirechan and Muirchu began the amplifications, continued with increasing proportions by the writers of the remaining Lives. As first of the evidences by which the purport of the original documents has been enlarged and modified to the great extent which will be presently disclosed, it ought not to be put forward at any disadvantage in form or substance as compared with them. It is therefore also given in its entirety, and with such aids to the reader in taking in its general tenor as a metrical version may confer. In this, the text and translation printed by Stokes in his "Goidelica," have been followed.

XXII.

The Fiacc Metrical Life.

(After A.D. 565.)

1.

Born in Nemthur was Patrick, as histories tell us.
At his age of sixteen he was brought under sorrow.

2.

His name at first, *Succat;* for his sire's, understand ye
'Twas *Calphurn mac Otid*, sprung from deacon *Odisse*.

3.

Six years in hard thraldom, man's victuals he ate not;
Four masters *Cothraige* obeyed in their households.

4.

Spake Victor to *Milchu's* thrall, "Over sea hie thee."
Where he planted his feet, on the rock rest their imprints.

5.

Over all the Alp mountains, over sea did he travel,
Till he tarried with *German*, in the south, in south Letha.*

---

* "Letha:" used generally for the continent of Europe, as Armorican Letha, Letha of Rome. The south of Gaul would appear to be here intended as comprising the Rhone delta and its islands (*post,* xxv.).

6.

In the Terrene sea islands he tarried, he pondered,
At reading the Canon, at study with *German*.

7.

To Erin he came by his Angel admonished,
In manifold visions to haste his returning.

8.

'Twas a good day for Erin the coming of Patrick;
He heard the young children from Focluth wood calling.

9.

They prayed to the holy one, that he would come to them,[*]
Come, and conduct them to life everlasting.

10.

For thus had their prophets foretold them the coming
Of a new time of peace would endure after Tara

11.

Lay desert and silent. The druids of *Laery*
Had told of his coming, had told of the Kingdom.

12.

Holy life led he still, strong expeller of evil,
Therefor do his merits shine high o'er the Nations.

---

[*] "Come to them:" till recently read as "They prayed that the holy one, traversing Letha, would come," &c. The more approved reading is now taken to be *lethu* = *cum illis*.

13.

The Hymns and Apocalypse and the Three Fifties
Sang he daily : baptizing, and praising God always.

14.

Nor allowed he the cold winter weather him hinder
From his nights in the water-pools; preaching, the daytime.

15.

In Slán well, by Boirche, he'd sing psalms a hundred
Ev'ry night in his suit to the High King of Angels,

16.

And would then take his sleep, on the bare rock reposing,
In his wet-dripping frock, with a stone for his pillow.

17.

He preached the glad Gospel ; he wrought many marvels ;
He healed halt and leper ; he raised the dead living.

18.

To the *Scoti* he preached it, with manifold labours,*
That they all might, at doomsday, attend round their
    Patron ;

19.

Emer's sons, sons of *Erimon*, all whom the Devil
Had theretofore shut in his great pit infernal,

---

* " With manifold labours :" till recently read as "After toiling through Letha."

20.

Till came their Apostle—as a swift wind his wending—
Preaching peace from Christ's cross, sixty years, to the *Feni.*

21.

There was darkness o'er Erin, they adored things of Faery;
They believed not the truth of the Trinity Godhead.

22.

In Armagh is Headship; long since life was in Emain;
A great church is Down; Tara—woe's me—a desert.

23.

When Patrick first sickened, he'd have fain gone to Macha;
By day came the Angel thereon to entreat him.

24.

He came south to Victor—it was he gave the summons—
The bush burned unburnt whereout Victor bespoke him,

25.

Saying "Headship to Macha" for which to Christ glory—
"But thou must to heaven, which grants thy petition,

26.

"That the hymn thou hast chosen shall be breast-plate of safety
To all who, at Doom, shall come round thee to judgment."

27.

He who gave him Communion, who survived him, was Tassach.
He had said he would come: and his words were accomplished.

28.

Night's shade set aside, there was light around unfading,
To a year's end was radiance, was one continual daylight.

29.

In the fight the son of Nun fought against them of Canaan,
When the sun stood still on Gibeon, as histories tell us,

30.

Though Joshua stayed the sun till the wicked were slaughtered.
More fitting was his light at death of holy Patrick.

31.

The clerks of Erin flocked to attend his funeral office.
The quiring angel's strain made them all sink down in slumber.

32.

The soul from Patrick's body, toil-worn, at last departed;
God's angels all the night sang around it unceasing.

33.

When Patrick departed, he went to the other Patrick,
And together they ascended to Jesus the Son of Mary.

34.

Humble Patrick, unblemished, much good did he accomplish.
In his service with Mary's Son, since first born in Nemthur.

XXIII. The *Fiacc* supplies the particular name of Patrick's birth-place, Nemthur, but affords no further clue to its local situation. It also for the first time introduces the name of Milchu, Patrick's bondmaster, and purports to give some account of Patrick's career after his escape from slavery and before entering on his Irish mission. Some time must have been spent by him in necessary clerical preparation; and this interval, passed over in the *Confessio*, is here accounted for by probationary studies pursued in the South of Europe under the tuition of Germanus, meaning, no doubt, the celebrated bishop of Auxerre of that name (xxii. 5, 6). During this period, apparently, Patrick is represented as having his Call from the children of Focluth (*ib.* 8, 9), an incident which, in the *Confessio*, is put at the home of his family in Britain (viii. 262-72); and this discrepancy cannot but detract from the credit of the *Fiacc* (11) and of the remaining authorities following it in this particular. It ascertains very clearly the epoch of the Irish mission of the Patrick it commemorates, which, in common with all the Lives, it represents as having taken place in the time of Leoghaire, son of Neil, A. D. 428-464. Its most noteworthy statement, however, is that intimating a plurality of Patricks (*ib.* 33), which shows that at least two personages of eminent sanctity were then recognised as having borne the name. To the evidences that Patricius was a title of office (Loc. Pat. 414), I add one example, the signature to the acts of the Council of Orange, A.D. 529, of P. M. F. Liberius V. C. et illustris præfectus prætorii Galliarum atque Patricius (Usher, 6, p. 26).

XXIV. The *Fiacc* has a Gloss and Scholium (*post*, xli.) the places of which, in order of date and authority, have not been determined. They appear to be subsequent to the Armagh Collections, and also to some of the "Colgan" Lives, inasmuch as identical matter of the Muirchu Life is found dispersed in the Scholium; and both Scholium and Gloss explain Nemthur as another name for Ailclyde, whereas the authors of Lives Two and Three repeat the Nemthur of *Fiacc*, without any attempt at identification. In this view the Armagh Collections come next in order after the text of the *Fiacc*, while the Gloss and Scholium of the latter fall into some place after Life Three.

XXV. What are known as the Annotations of Tirechan in the Book of Armagh are, as has been seen (*sup.* xvii.), presumably older than the Life by Muirchu; and will first be noticed for some light they may possibly throw on the subject of there having been more Patricks than one (*sup.* xxiii.). "I have found," he says (Hog. Doc. de S⁰⁰. P. 57), "in Bishop Ultan's book four names for Patrick, that is, *Magon*, or the renowned; *Succat*, who is Patrick—*qui est Patricius*—and *Cothirthiacus*, because he served in four households of the Magi." Bringing Patrick at once to the field of his missionary employment, Tirechan affords no information as to his place of origin. His condensed introductory chapter may be regarded as a summary of the beliefs respecting the pre-missionary life of Patrick which were in current acceptance in Ireland about the middle of the seventh century. Having related the story of his captivity in the service of Milchu, in his first chapter, he thus proceeds:—

"Then, however, the Angel of the Lord visited him in his dreams, on the heights of Skirte (Skirry), near to Sliebh Miss. And this was the Angel's last command: 'Behold, thy ship is ready: arise and journey (*ambula*),' and he (the Angel) departed from him up to heaven; and he arose and journeyed (*ambulavit*) according to the command of the Lord's Angel, Victor by name. In his seventeenth year was he captured, led away and sold into Ireland; in his twenty-second year it was vouchsafed to him to leave his toils with the Magi. Seven other years he journeyed (*ambulavit*), and sailed the seas (*in fluctibus*), in plains and mountain-valleys, throughout Gaul and all Italy, and in the islands which are in the Terrene Sea, as he himself has said in his narrative (*commemoratio*) of his labours. And he was thirty years in one of these islands, which is called *Aralanensis*, as Bishop Ultan testified to me. But all that happened to him you may find written in the distinct history of him. These [matters which I am now about to relate] are his latest *mirabilia*, concluded and happily accomplished (*finita atque feliciter facta*) in the fifth year of the reign (*in V. regni anno*) of Loigire Mac Neill" (Hog. Doc. 57, c. 1).

He then relates the missionary *acta* of Patrick, extending over seventy-two years (c. 53), which, if they were finished at the time stated, would throw back his advent to A.D. 359. The other relevant passage is from his 56th chapter (Hog. Doc. 89):

"In the thirteenth year of the Emperor Theodosius, Patrick is sent [as] Bishop, for the instruction (*ad doctrinam*) of the Scoti, by Bishop Celestine, Pope of

E

Rome: which Celestine was forty-seventh Bishop from the Apostle Peter in Rome city. Paladius is first sent [as] Bishop, who was called Patrick for his other name (*sup.* xxiii.; *post*, xlviii.), who suffered martyrdom amongst the Scoti, as holy men of old testify. Then the Second Patrick is sent by the Angel of God, Victor by name, and by Pope Celestine; through whom all Ireland believed, who gave baptism to almost all of it. . . . All which things, in God accomplished, have been gathered together by the most skilful of our ancients."

There are four remarkable passages connecting some Patrick with a precedent Christian institution in Ireland in Tirechan. Coming to Coleraine, after crossing the river Bann, on his return from his visitation of Connaught, Patrick imparts his blessing to that place, " in quo fuit episcopus" (Hog. Doc., 86). In Find Moy of Hy Maine, Patrick finds the cross which the Christian mother had planted by mistake over the sepulchre of the pagan buried beside her son (Hog. Doc., 83). In Tir Erril he discovers the altar (Hog. Doc., 69) which, the Tripartite explains, lay with its glass chalices hidden in a cave in Dumagraid. At Achadgower, in Mayo, there came to him a pious maiden, Mathona, a nun, sister, or relative of Benignus, who assisted at the episcopal ordination of her brother Senach. Senach appears to have made certain stipulations regarding his orders (Hog. Doc., 80; Hennessy, *apud* Cus.), and the result is, in the language of Tirechan, " missam Patricii acceperunt," all which tend to favour the inference that, besides the author of the *Confessio*, some other and later Patrick has been commemorated in the Lives.

XXVI. The *Muirchu* Life, since the discovery of the Brussels manuscript, which makes up its chapters missing from the Book of Armagh, may now be considered as a document of greater importance than even the Annotations of Tirechan. A few years ago it became known that a vellum manuscript Life of Patrick existed in the Royal Library at Brusssels which appeared to correspond with the *Muirchu* Life, so far as it is found in the Book of Armagh. We should not have had this valuable identification of the perfect twelfth century copy with the imperfect ninth century transcript of this seventh century compilation, if our late brother Academician, Sir William Betham, had not, in what must now be deemed a happy moment, ventured on the editing, however imperfectly, of the Book of Armagh (*Antiquarian Researches*, Dublin). He puts this venerable record, so far as it relates to St. Patrick, substantially before the world, and enabled the learned men who at Brussels continue the work of the Bollandi Fratres, to recognise the identity of the Life in their Royal Library with the Life by Muirchu in the Armagh Codex in Trinity College Library here. This has led to a most careful comparison of the two texts by the Rev. Edward Hogan, S.J., to whom we are also indebted for the "Documenta de Sancto Palricio" above referred to, printed at Brussels in 1884. Dr. Whitley Stokes had already, in his *Goidelica*, translated the Irish passages, in which the imperfections of Sir William Betham's Essay chiefly betrayed itself. Mr. Hogan extends his work to all the contents of this part of the

Codex, both Latin and Irish, and, in the first six chapters of the *Muirchu* Life, supplies us with the matter which, undoubtedly, at one time, existed on the folio now missing from our own Book.

XXVII. In the newly-acquired part of the Life, Muirchu, as regards Patrick's place of nativity, grounds himself on the *Confessio* with an addition which may help towards the better ascertainment of the site. The scribe presents the *Bannave Tabernice* of the *Confessio* in the dislocated form *Ban navem thabur indecha*, where the added *decha* may recall the Dakenclud of the Dunbarton terminus of Græme's Dyke, as described by John Major (Hist. Maj. Brit. l. i. ci.). He then proceeds with other matter equally remarkable, "quem vicum constanter, indubitanterque comperimus esse *ventre*." Here may be recognised the source of Probus's statement in Life Five of the Trias, "quem vicum constanter indubitanterque comperimus esse *Neutrix* provinciam," which has caused so may fine intelligences, in search of Patrick's birth-place, to cross the English Channel into the Gaulish province of *Neustria*. Every one acquainted with common palæographic difficulties knows how often it occurs that *u* and *n* have been mistaken for one another. Thus Dunbarton, in the old Welsh dialogue between Taliesin and Merlin (Skene F. B.), appears as Neutur. In the Myvirian Archæology, the editor has read it Nentur. In both shapes it seems to be the equivalent of Fiacc's *Nemthor*, whatever that name may originally have been.

XXVIII. In these recovered chapters, Muirchu, following the *Confessio*, conducts Patrick from captivity to his family in Britain, and plainly declares that, in his view, this was insular Britain, by bringing him thence to Gaul over sea, "transnavigato mari dextro Britannico."

XXIX. The Brussels complemental matter supplies another incident in the *Muirchu* Life, which may be noted as one of the points of later departure from the sequence of events recorded in the *Confessio*. He has a chapter (3) on a second captivity, which, according to his account, Patrick, after his escape to Britain, suffered "ab alienigenis." This adventure has been expanded by one of the subsequent Life writers (*post*, xlii.) into a sea voyage from the Boyne to Bordeaux, with a twenty-eight days' journey through French desert (viii. 255 *n*.), conducting Patrick to his kinsman St. Martin of Tours. The whole appears to be a parasitic growth, and to depend from that one point in the story of the *Confessio* where Patrick uses the words, "et iterum post annos multos adhuc capturam dedi." At this point there is a hiatus in the Book of Armagh. Patrick having described his nightmare in the desert, and stated what seems to have been his belief that it was Christ who, within him, made use of his, Patrick's, voice to exclaim "Helias," proceeds to justify that belief from Scripture "*Sicut in euangelio dixit dominus non uos estis*," followed by the unconnected words, "*multos adhuc capturam dedi*." The Bodleian and other texts supply what is here plainly wanting, namely, "*qui loquimini, sed spiritus Patris vestri qui loquitur in vobis. Et iterum post annos*," which complete the sense. This has been taken as if Patrick were here writing in reference to a bodily captivity. But they who, following Muirchu, so understood the texts, have overlooked the "adhuc," which, in its context, imports a captivity still continuing. Patrick certainly was not in bodily bondage when he wrote the *Confessio;* whence it must be concluded that his words, if they be not scriptural quotation, are necessarily to be understood as of a spiritual captivity, such as that of "aged Paul now also a prisoner of the Lord." Indeed the expression "et iterum" is so often used in the *Confessio* as introductory of scriptural citation when a further text is vouched in support of a preceding one, that, if the words in question could be at all adapted to the language of the Epistle to Philemon, such would be a welcome version of the passage. But they can only by a great stretch of adaptation be so considered; and the incurring of a spiritual bondage remains as the preferable construction. It was the first occasion on which he had experienced what he conceived to be the presence of an indwelling coercer of his will, to obedience to whose promptings all his subsequent life was to be conformed; and this probably will be received as the meaning conveyed in "eâ nocte primâ." That he believed himself to be subject to this kind of bondage, even up to the time of his death, was the tradition amongst the writers of the Lives. "When

Patrick first sickened, he had fain lain in Macha" (xxii. 23), but such was not the divine will. "Alas," he says to Victor, who tells him this request was denied, "my captivity is even to the end; since I cannot so much as choose for myself the place of my burial" (Vita 3ª, c. 88).

XXX. This part of the *Confessio*, therefore, it may be affirmed gives no support to the theory of more than one captivity in the ordinary sense of the word, and is quite consistent with the completion of Patrick's whole journey within the predicted two months, when, after the six years of his detention in Ireland—comparatively few as contrasted with the life-long duration of his other kind of captivity—he found himself again at home in Britain, agreeably to the first prediction, which, it may be observed, all the other interpretations necessarily contradict, "*cito iturus ad patriam vestram et terram.*"

XXXI. Having described Patrick's return to his family, as in the *Confessio*, Muirchu, in the fifth and sixth chapters of the new matter supplied to us by these *Complementa*, passes into a condensed and somewhat abrupt continuation of the narrative:—

"And many visions were there shown him. And he was of the age of thirty years, as the apostle says (et cetera), to (the measure of) the fulness of Christ, (when) going forth to the Apostolic seat, to visit and honor (it) even as the head of all the Churches of the whole world, in order that, understanding already the divine and sacred mysteries whereto God had called him, he should learn, understand, fulfil, preach, and confer the divine favor on the extern nations, converting them to the faith of Christ."

From which it may be collected that, in Muirchu's view, Patrick had at this time acquired the knowledge of his ecclesiastical office, but before entering on it desired to testify his respect to the Holy See, and, it may be inferred, to obtain its sanction for his undertaking:—

"Having therefore sailed across the southern sea of Britain, in order to proceed across the Gaulish Alps by the accepted (the ordinary?) route (*accepto itinere*), at their extremity, which he had in his heart proposed to take, he found a certain most holy prince bishop and high duke at Alsiodor (Auxerre) city, with whom (he remained in study)," &c. "And, having there spent a long time as, forty years according to some, thirty according to others, his old and right trusty (angel) Victoricus by name, who [here the Armagh text begins] had predicted to him in Ireland all things before they came to pass, visited him with frequent visions, telling him the time was now arrived when he should come (hither) and, with the net of the evangel, fish for those rude and savage peoples for whose instruction God had destined him; and there it was said to him in a vision, *The sons and daughters of the Wood of Focluth call thee*," &c.

Where the growing disregard of the authority of the *Confessio* may be observed in the transfer of the place of his call from his home in Britain to Auxerre in Gaul.

Then follows, in both texts, the incident of the death of

Palladius, leading to Patrick's proceeding at once on his Irish mission, without waiting to complete his intended journey to Rome. The statement of Palladius' mission is substantially as above given by Tirechan (xxv.), save that Pope Celestine does not appear in it. Patrick, on Victor's summons, sets out on his "inceptum iter." Whether this was for Rome or for Ireland is not stated. On his way he receives intelligence of the death of Palladius at a place the situation of which has given rise to much speculation. It is doubtfully called *Ebmoria* in the Armagh, and distinctly *Curbia* in the Brussels, Codex. If the "inceptum iter" were for Ireland, *Curbia* would seem the better reading, for Corbie is on the route northward from Auxerre. If for Rome, the site of *Ebmoria* should be looked for on the "acceptum iter" by the extremity of the Gaulish Alps. These, in Irish geography, are the mountain chains of Auvergne and Languedoc, in which the Loire has its sources. At their eastern extremity, "ad extremum," the valley of the Rhone gives access to the Terrene or Mediterranean Sea. Here, in the delta of the Rhone, is the island of Arles (*Arelato*), to which reference is found above in Tirechan, under the name Aralanensis (xxv.), but which has its true name Arelatensis in the Fourth Life (*post*, xxxix.), and being also known as the Insula Cameracenis, has been satisfactorily identified by Colgan with the modern Camargue. A British connexion had been established at Arles by the *pseudo* Emperor Constantine, about 407, if it did not exist before, and there will be nothing locally improbable in voyages from thence to Italy ascribed to Patrick in other Lives. Wherever the disciples with news of Palladius' death, met Patrick, his further proceedings, according to Muirchu, were taken with great promptitude.

"Patrick and those who were with him changing their route, turned aside (*declinaverunt iter*) to a certain wondrous man and chief bishop, Amathorex by name, living in a neighbouring place, and there the holy Patrick, knowing what would befall, received the episcopal grade from the holy bishop Mathorex. Auxilius also was ordained, and (so were) Isernine, and others of lower degree, on the same day as holy Patrick. Then the venerable traveller, &c., took ship and reached Britain, and omitting all occasions of delay, save the common requirements of the road, for no man can seek the Lord by dallying, with all speed and a favouring wind crosses over sea."

XXXII. The *Muirchu* Life is divided into chapters. A short index to the headings of the several chapters is found in both copies. One of these, No. 28, is conversant with the Coroticus incident (*sup.* xiii.). The text of the chapter, missing from the Armagh Codex, is present in the Brussels copy. It makes *Corictic* (*Coirthech* in Lib. Arm.) a British king, and the entitlement of the chapter in both examples is "De conflictu Patricii adversum *Coirthech* regem *Aloo*." Alo-clotha is the form in which Ailclyde is presented in the older Irish annals, as *Alofind* for Elphin in the Book of Armagh. There is no other royal seat in insular or continental Britain compounded in *Ail* but Ailclyde. It is, therefore, matter of cogency to conclude that, in the seventh century, the Coroticus of Patrick's epistle was regarded as king of Ailclyde the capital of the kingdom of the Strathclyde Britons. In the Welsh additions to the *Historia Britonum* of Nennius is a list of these Strathclyde kings, including the name of *Ceretic guledec*, that is, *Dux* or *Imperator*, the native designation given to various British *reguli* who from time to time usurped the imperial purple. The document is referred to A.D. 977 (Skene, An. P. & S. xcv. 15). It purports to trace the pedigree of Run Map Artgal through fifteen generations, to *Ceretic guledec*. Run was reigning in Ailclyde A.D. 878, which, at thirty years to the generation, would put the middle age of *Ceretic* about A.D. 428. Other computations of the same kind, grounded on the dates or intermediate names in the list, would bring him down to A.D. 470 or 480, in full agreement with the accepted Patrician chronology. This list, however, is an instructive example of the uncertainty attending the thirty years canon, when applied to any but long and well-authenticated lines of descent. Among other issue of Ceretic, set forth in it, are Rydderch Hael and his father Tudwal Tutclud, both mentioned by Adamnan, and of known historic dates. Ridderch, fifth in descent, reigning A.D. 573, would put Ceretic, the great-great-grandfather about A.D. 423. Tudwal, a generation nearer, is made by the author of the Life of Ninian cotemporary with a Ninian, who must be taken as the second of the name, and who flourished at Whiterne about

A.D. 520 (Usher, 6, 585). He is also made by the author of the Life of Kentigern, cotemporary with Darerca, the supposed sister of St. Patrick, who died A.D. 518 (*ib.* 584). If Tudwal were reigning at any time so shortly after the death of Patrick, commonly assigned to A.D. 493, Ceretic, his great grandfather, could hardly have been the reigning cotemporary of the same Patrick. Nor do the difficulties arising on the epoch of Coroticus stop here. There is another copy of the Run pedigree, compiled about A.D. 1300 (Sk. F. B. 167), amongst the Hengwrt Manuscripts. In this, while the generation numbers are the same, the names between the *Guledec* and Tudwal differ, suggesting the loss of one or more generations, while the *Guledec* is named Maxen, as if *Ceretic* were, *alio nomine*, *Maxen Wledeg*, or that Maximus raised by the Britons to the Imperial rank, who reigned A.D. 383-9. In reference to him, there is a statement by Johannes Major, not irrelevant to this enquiry, though not vouched for by any other authority. Having described the last constructed Roman wall between Abercornie and Dakenclud, and stated that it ran 8,000 paces further to the North than the old line of Agricola, he goes on to say, regarding the additional land so gained, "hanc terram Maximus dux suo regno adjecit" (Hist. Maj. Brit. l. 1, c. 1). On these data the epoch of Coroticus, and of the Patrick from whom he received the epistle, will appear earlier or later, according as the mind of the reader may be swayed in either direction by the other evidences.

XXXIII. The Book of Armagh contains matter supplemental to the compilations of Tirechan. The Codex here has the appearance of a commonplace book of undigested material, partly in Latin and partly in Irish. In that portion which is in the Irish language occurs an account of the proceedings of Isernine, above referred to (xxxi.). He is here identified with an Irish bishop, Idh, and represented as engaged in a proceeding not easily to be reconciled with the statement of his having been the cotemporary of Germanus. Patrick and he had sailed by different routes for the same destination. Patrick had arrived by way of a port on the eastern, Isernine by one on the southern, coast. Isernine is represented as visiting, first, his own kindred of the Cothraige, a small tribe in the present county of Carlow. Thence he proceeds into the southern borders of Wicklow where he converts and baptizes the seven sons of Cathbod. This innovation, it is represented, was displeasing to the then king of Leinster, namely Enna Cennsalagh, who proscribed the converts. They, accompanied by Isernine, went into exile in another part of the country, where Patrick subsequently joined them, and by his interest with Crimthan, son of Enna, obtained their pardon. Enna Cennsalagh was a personage having a well-defined place in Irish history. He overthrew the monarch, Eochaid Muimedon at the battle of Cruachan Clœnta, about A.D. 358. He appears to have been then a man of many exploits, and is said (O'Curry, 493) to have warred against the Ulster kingdom at or before the destruction of Emania. The statement respecting him in the Book of Leinster is that he was cotemporary of Enna Nia, father of the first Dunlang king of Leinster, and great-great-grand father of that second Dunlang, whose sons Iollan and Ailill Patrick is stated in the Lives to have baptized at Naas: Enna Genselac*h* da*n* agus Enna Nia comamser doib andís *unde* lugair d*ix*i*t*. Mair drecuin drecuin da Enna húi nathaig nuadat nascad giallu gaedel necht. "The same time then for both Enna Genselach and Enna Nia, as Lugair said : Great dragons of dragons are the two Ennas, descendants of the wounding hostage-binder of the Gael, Nuadu Necht" (L.L. 316 *b*). He was fourth in descent from Cathir Mor, whose death is put, at latest, in A.D. 177, and must apparently have been long past middle age when the conversion of the sons of Cathbod took place. If we can credit our Irish pedigrees, the sons of Cathbod were eighth in descent from Cucorb king of Leinster (Loc. Pat. tab. 1), whose death is put at A.D. 119. This would make their probable period A.D. 360. With all allowances for lives of exceptional duration, we cannot bring down the actors in these affairs to the post-Palladian period without excessive straining of probabilities and many serious misgivings.

XXXIV. These Additions further throw light on some obscurities respecting the epoch of Fiacc, nephew of Dubtach Maccu Lugair, ordained bishop by Patrick on his journey into Enna's territory of Hy Kinsela. In c. 51 of Tirechan (Hog. Doc. 88) Patrick, after his ordination of Fiacc, on his way to Munster, is represented as also baptizing the sons of Dunlang, meaning, in the common acceptance of the Life-writers, the above mentioned Iollan and Ailill, the sons of his convert Dunlang the second, king of Leinster, about A.D. 450. That it was the elder Dunlang, however, who is here referred to by Tirechan, may be thought probable from the fact that he had at least seven sons, which is not reported of his great-grandson Dunlang the second; and that the Irish-Latin additions to Tirechan, after the statement respecting the sons of Cathbod (*supra*) go on to say, "ranic Patraic iarsuidiu (Patrick came afterwards) et crediderunt sibi (vii.) filii Dunlangi" (Hog. Doc. 103), implying very persuasively that the ordination of Fiacc, and the conversions of the sons of Cathbod and of Dunlang, were nearly contemporaneous. Fiacc, after his ordination, remained (*congabt*) at his first church at Minbeg, on the borders of Wicklow and Carlow, until sixty of his community died (*contorchartar*) there. An angel afterwards commanded him to remove to Sletty, on the opposite side of the Barrow, where his resurrection was to be. Fiacc would not, unless Patrick in person should come to lay out his new church, which Patrick afterwards did (Hog. Doc. 107, 8). This has the appearance of a translation of relics, after Fiacc's remains had been interred in Minbig for a lengthened period. One of the traditions respecting him and his son Fiachra purports so to represent the fact. Colgan (Tr. Th. 185, *n*. 37) cites this from the Calendar of Cashel, " Fiacrius filius

Fiachi, et ambo quiescunt in Minbeg;" repeated by Cathal Maguire in his Martyrology, " Fiacrius filius est Fiaci, et est (*sup.* xvi.) cum eo simul in Minbeag, nempe in cella parva quæ est in sylva inter Cluain Mor Maedoc et Aghad Abhail, in qua et sanctus Fiacus jacet " (Loc· Pat. 197). Great difficulty has been experienced in co-ordinating Fiacc with Patrick and the younger Dunlang; and Todd (Book of Hymns, 292) in making out a late enough date for Fiacc, has been obliged to insert some questionable and several surmised steps in his pedigree.

XXXV. The lives remaining to be examined are the Second to the Seventh inclusive in the Trias, reckoning under the last its duplicate known as the Irish Tripartite. All of them, for the reasons assigned (xx.), are taken as posterior in date of compilation to the *Fiacc*, and to the collections of Tirechan and the Life by Muirchu in the Book of Armagh. As amongst themselves, the only departure from the order given them that I would venture to suggest, would be a transposition of Six and Seven— that is, a postponement of the Life by Jocelyn (A.D. 1182) to the Tripartite, the direct internal evidences of which do not come lower down than A.D. 897 (Hennessy, *apud* Cus., p. 466). These with the Fifth Life, bearing the name of Probus as author, and referable by very pregnant indications to the tenth century (Tr. Th. 61, 2 ; 64, 38), are the only ones of the series which afford clear evidences of their periods. Two, Three, and Four have

LIFE TWO. 81

been arranged by Colgan in the order of seniority of their supposed authors, Patrick junior, Benignus, and Eleran the Wise; but these early origins, for the reasons above given (*sup.* xvi.), cannot now be sustained, and for the further reasons also premised (*sup.* xix.), must all be postponed in date to the Life by Muirchu. No better sequence, however, irrespective of positive dates, than that given them by Colgan can be suggested, especially as Two and Three appear to ground themselves on Irish originals, and preserve, imbedded in their Latin text, several examples of that kind of fossil material.

XXXVI. Life Two then follows *Fiacc* in making Nemthor the place of Patrick's birth, but adds nothing express to our knowledge of where *Nemthor* is, beyond what may be inferred from its use of the language of Muirchu in bringing Patrick from the home of his family into Gaul by crossing the southern British Sea (Tr. Th., 13, c. xxi.); whence its author must be concluded to have supposed the home insular.

It also with the metrical Life attaches itself unconformably to the narrative of the *Confessio* at the point where Patrick is told to take shipping for home, and marks expressly the discrepancy which in the *Fiacc* is only inferential (*sup.* xxii. 4, 5): " Ecce, navis tua parata est, ut peteret (peteres) Italiam, ut ibi per sanctam Scripturam disciplinandus esses" (Tr. Th., 12, c. xvii.). Its staple, like that of all the other remaining Lives, is drawn from Muirchu, prefaced by numerous *mirabilia* of

F

the Infancy, here apparently for the first time introduced, and supplemented by some particulars, also appearing to be here of primary introduction, relating to Patrick's *acta* and cotemporaries. Having related his call (c. xxi.), which, with the *Confessio* it makes in Britain, "cum parentibus suis," it takes up the narrative of Muirchu, and conducts him, as above, across the southern sea of Britain to Germanus, with whom he reads for thirty years "in insula Arelanensi" (c. xxii.), being, doubtless, the Island of Arles above referred to (*sup.* xxxi.). Then, again following Muirchu, it relates the mission of Palladius by Pope Celestine, his failure, and death in *Forddun*, or, as others say, his martyrdom (c. xxiv.). Here also it introduces, apparently for the first time, the name of Nathi filius Garrchon, who, on Palladius' arrival "in fines Lageniensium," offered him some opposition. After which it interposes somewhat abruptly in Muirchu's narrative a short but pregnant chapter (xxv.) in these words :—" Patrick, sent by the same Pope Celestine to Ireland, came to the mouth of a certain river, the *Deac* (*Inbhir Deagadh*, Wicklow). But the aforesaid wicked nobleman, Nathi, who previously had withstood Palladius, opposed the blessed Patrick also and his doctrine. But Sinell, son of Findcath, through the preaching of the holy Patrick, believed in Almighty God, and first amongst the Scots was baptized of holy Patrick, wherefore he (Patrick) bestowed his blessing on him and on his seed." Patrick then, proceeding northward into Ulster, makes his first convert Dichu, *Primus Scotorum per Patricum*

Confessus (*ib.* c. xxix.) ; and afterwards, returning to Wicklow, is received by the grandson, and gives his blessing to the infant great-grandson, of Sinell.

Two first converts are certainly suggestive of different and successive missions; and if Dichu be properly placed 63 in his table of descent, Sinell being 59, one must recognize a great difference in time.

XXXVII. Both Nathi and Sinell are well-known names in what is called the Dal Messincorb genealogy, preserved in the Book of Leinster and elsewhere, and lately published from these sources by the Rev. J. F. Shearman (Loc. Pat., Tab. i.). Sinell is, in all the extant examples of this pedigree, eighth in descent from Cucorb king of Leinster. Cucorb's epoch is ascertained by that of Fedlimedh Reactmar king of Ireland, A.D. 113-119, by whom he was slain. His fourth son was Messincorb, amongst whose descendants are found Findcath, Sinell, and Sinell's cotemporary, Nathi. Here it will be well to preserve a judicious observation of Colgan, the truth and appositeness of which all students of these genealogical tables will readily acknowledge. " Nostros historices quando non texunt genealogias, solere sæpè usurpare nomen filii latè, pro nepote, aliove descendente" (Tr. Th., 18, n. 35). For Sinell, in the pedigree, is not son, but great-grandson of Findcath ; being son of Conall, son of Cucongelt, son of Findcath, son of Garrchu, son of Fothad, son of Eochaid Lamderg, son of Messincorb, son of Cucorb; and, at the generally accepted rate of thirty years to a generation, should, together with his cotemporary Nathi, if the pedigree be right, be concluded to have flourished about A.D. 360, synchronously with Enna Cennsalagh and the sons of Cathbod, who, it will be remembered, are brought within the first influences of the Patrician mission by the supplementer of Tirechan (*sup.* xxxiii.). All deductions, however, of this kind, are subject to the possibility that steps in the pedigree may have been lost; and Shearman, deeming the post-Palladian date, which he considered the true one, to be irreconcilable with this epoch for Sinell, has felt himself justified in suggesting—"Some generations are wanting between Garrchu, *circa* 200, and Findcath" (Loc. Pat., Tab. i., No. 55). If three generations, indeed, could be so interpolated, Sinell would be brought down to post-Palladian times; but no ground for such an alteration of the text can be suggested save that of conformity to accepted ideas.

XXXVIII. Life Three adopts the statement and language of Life Two as regards Nemthor and the early *mirabilia*. It follows substantially the story of the *Confessio* up to Patrick's escape, his return to his parents, and his call by the Voices from Focluth, which it gives in the Irish, *hoch! aillilo furtaich* (c. xx.). It then takes up the thread of Muirchu's relation, and conducts him to St. Germanus, at Auxerre. In common with all the remaining Lives, however, it breaks up the thirty or forty years assigned by Muirchu to Patrick's studies under Germanus, and, after some time spent at Auxerre, transfers him to the tuition of St. Martin of Tours (Tr. Th. 22, xxii.), thence to the Tamerensian (Camerensian) island, and thence to Rome, where he receives another call (Tr. Th. 22, xxiii.). This transfer to the tuition of Martin involves an insuperable anachronism. Martin had died before A.D. 418, the date of Germanus' call to ecclesiastical orders. In describing these travels it introduces apparently for the first time, those anomalies in continental geography which here and in all the remaining Lives, bespeak a date in times of diminishing enlightenment, and have occasioned extreme embarrassment to successive commentators. Patrick, at Rome, hears the voice of the angel, "'Go thou to the island Hibernia, and aid them who invoke thee.' And Patrick said, 'I will not go until,' &c. And the angel led him to Mount Arnon *ar muir letha* (on the sea of Letha) on a rock of the Tyrrene Sea, in a city which is called Capua" (Tr. Th. 23, xxv.). Elsewhere this mountain is called Armon, Morion, and Narnchin (Lit. Ængus. L. Br.), and is placed somewhere in the neighbourhood of the Arelatensian island; whence it may be surmised that Capua is either a geographical blunder, or that the name may have been borne by some city of Provence, as that of "The Rome of Gaul" was borne by Arles.

As regards epoch, this Life, as well as the next, ascribes the martyrdom of Odhran, the Saint's charioteer, to a person far out of the range of any Patrician chronology, namely, Folige, from whom the Hy Failge, "a quo orti sunt alii Folgi," that is, Rossa Foilge, eldest son of Cathir Mor, whose date would be early in the third century. The subsequent Lives correct this anachronism by introducing a Foilge Bearraidh (sl. A.D. 501, Q.M.) as the murderer; but, assuming Life Three to be of earlier compilation, it is worth remark that it represents Foilge as having been revisited "post multum temporis" by Patrick, affording another instance of successive *acta*, at long intervals, ascribed to one or more of the name. The body of Foilge had in the meantime been inhabited by the demon, and on being summoned to Patrick's presence, his dry bones only are found in his house (Tr. Th. 25, c. lix.). The remainder of the Third Life appears to be drawn from Muirchu and Tirechan.

XXXIX. Life Four begins with a tradition that the family of Patrick was of Jewish descent, and reached their settlement in Strath-clyde, "in qua terra conceptus et natus est" (Tr. Th. 35, c. i.), by way of Armorica "juxta mare Thyrrenum," showing that in the writer's judgment there were several Armoricas, one on the southern as well as the better known Armorica on the northern sea-board of Gaul. Having suggested the interpretation "turris cœlestis" for *Nemthor*, and given the current version of *Campus Tabernix*, he adds, "Britannica autem lingua *Campus Tabern* idem campus tabernaculorum dicitur," probably referring to the *Moy Tabern* of old Irish Tuatha de Danaan tradition, whose site on independent grounds, is put in this region by O'Flaherty

(Ogygia l.iii., c.xxiii.). The story attaches itself somewhat unconformably to the narrative of the *Confessio* : " Ecce navistua parata est; tempus namque adest ut in sanctis litteris docearis " (Tr. Th., 37, c. xxi.). It then conducts Patrick, " Elevato velo, prospero flatu, ad Britanicos sinus " (c. xxiii.), to his parents, where he has his call, and whence he proceeds across the southern British Sea to Saint Germanus, first at Auxerre, and afterwards in the Arelatensian island, where he has a further call, again repeated in Rome, whither he proceeds by sea, " per mare Thyrrenum navigando transivit " (c. xxix.), and so back again to Ireland, " recto transitu per Italiam Galliasque." The writer cites the *Confessio*, and, in two instances, from texts not now known to exist. In one of these, Patrick is made to state that his mother was *Concessa* (Tr. Th., 15, c. i.) ; and in the other (37, c. xvii.) to supply an additional example of the psychological experiences of his youth. In this passage, relating his life in the wilds while herding the flocks of Milchu, he goes on to say, *Audiebam quosdam ex spiritibus psallentes in me, et nesciebam qui essent*. " I heard certain of the spirits within me singing psalms, and I knew not who they might be " (*ante*. viii., 276).

It cannot be said that the Fourth Life supplies anything from which an earlier epoch than that usually ascribed to Patrick can definitely be inferred. It brings him in contact (c. lxxvii.) with the Foilge above-mentioned, but without the story of the dry bones. There may be more matter for reasonable speculation on this head in its statement (c. lxxviii.) that, on a certain occasion Patrick was accompanied on his progress through the borders of Ossory by bishops Ibar and Ailbe. It would be too wide a subject here, to enter on an examination of the grounds on which the obits of these ecclesiastics have been determined in our annals, but I do not desire, in passing the topic by, to be understood as yielding convinced assent to the late date assigned.

XL. The Fifth Life, in two books, a work well ascertained to the tenth century, bears the name of Probus as author. The writer is manifestly Irish (Tr. Th., 61, *n.* 2). It is to be regretted that, having ascertained, "indubitanter," that *Bannave Tabernix regionis* is *Nentrix provinciam ubi olim gigantes habitasse dicuntur*, he does not more distinctly state where Nentria is. He makes Patrick, however, a Briton, intimating at the same time that he himself writes in these islands:—"*Hic in Britanniis natus.*" He contradicts the *Confessio* in putting Patrick's call at Mount Hermon, near the Terrene Sea (c. xviii.). His relation of the capture is extremely confused, but seems to show that he understood *Arimuric* in the same sense as the author of Life Four, that is, as a designation of any maritime district. The word, indeed, continued to be so used by Irish writers down to the time of O'Flaherty, who dates the Epistle Dedictory of his Ogygia "Aremoricâ Galviensi." Having stated that Patrick was born " his in Britanniis," he proceeds:—"Cumque adhuc esset in patria cum patre

Calfurnio et matre Concessa, in civitate eorum *Arimuric*, facta est seditio magna in partibus illis. Nam filii Rethmiti Regis de Britannia vastantes *Arimuric*, et alia circumposita loca, jugulaverunt Calpurnium et uxorem ejus Concessam, filiosque eorum, Patricium, &c.— abducentes Hiberniam ingressi sunt et vendiderunt Patricium Milchoni regi," &c.—which can hardly be otherwise read than that while Patrick was still in his own country with his father and mother (i.e., *hic in Britanniis*) in their seaside abode (*civitate Aremorica*) the misfortune in question befell them. Obviously the passage is either an inaccurate copy of the corresponding statements in the scholium on the metrical Life, or the latter is an improvement on it or some similar account.

XLI. The statement of the Scholiast, whatever be its true place in the sequence (*ante*, xxiv.), is more definite. He alleges the identity of *Nemthor* with Ailclyde, and accounts for Patrick having been carried off from Lethanian Aremorica, in which, if we accept his authority, we should conclude *Bannave Taberniæ* to be situate, by the circumstance that he had accompanied his family from Strathclyde thither. Contrasting the one story with the other, the less exact will probably be regarded as the older. Whichever be the original, these passages no doubt are the foundation of all that has been conjectured regarding Patrick's Armorican connexion, and his birth among the continental Britons, although both explicitly exclude the latter inference.

XLII. Probus interposes a third captivity between Patrick's return to his family in insular Britain and his first departure on his Irish mission, conducting him by way of Bordeaux to St. Martin at Tours, from whom he receives the tonsure and ordination; thence to the "Eremitas et Solitarios nudis pedibus"; thence to the Island between the mountains and the sea, from which he goes to Mount Hermon, and is there ordained presbyter by Bishop Senior, whose city, we are informed, " vallata est septem muris (Tr. Th., 48, xvii.). A frequent source of error in Irish transcription arises from the confusion between the characters or sigla expressing six and seven (*sé* and *secht*); and a six-walled city, *Sixfours* the *Hexafrourai* of the Massilian colonists, does, indeed, exist within no great distance of Arles, and may be the place referred to. There is, however, notwithstanding much obscurity in the account of these peregrinations, a general consistency which forbids our ascribing it to mere invention, and few readers will rise from a perusal of Probus without the persuasion that some apostolic missionary of the Irish— whether Palladius Patrick, Senior Patrick, or Patrick the author of the *Confessio*—did, some time in the fourth or beginning of the fifth century, sojourn for purposes of ecclesiastical training in those regions bordering the Terrene Sea on the southern coast of Gaul. It is to this region Probus, in continuing disregard of the *Confessio*, transfers the Call of the children of Focluth Wood, and brings Patrick thence in prompt obedience to it on his mission to the Irish. Coming hither as a simple presbyter, and without commision, Patrick finds himself unsuccessful, and resolves to seek necessary authority at Rome (Tr. Th., 43, c. xix.). At this point Probus, resuming the narrative of Muirchu, " transnavigato vero mari Britannico" (Hog. Doc., 24, c. 25), conducts Patrick to Germanus, and proceeds with the remaining incidents of his hearing of Palladius' mission and death, and of his return hither, and missionary *acta*, as already related. These various captivities and double mission taken in connexion with the two Patricks of the " Fiacc " Life (xxiii.) are certainly suggestive of blended sets of *acta* of several persons living at different epochs.

XLIII. The Tripartite, or Life Seven, is the most copious repertory of all; and, from the fact that the first elements of almost all its matter may be found in the Book of Armagh, either recorded at length or indicated in the rough index (Hog. Doc. 110-16) to names of persons and places at the end of Tirechan in that collection, there can be little doubt that, whatever be the date of its compilation in its present form, most of its substance is drawn from traditions which were current before the compilation of the Armagh Codex. It may, therefore, be of an authority equal to that of any of the antecedent Lives. Its testimony on the question of birthplace is explicit, that Patrick was born at Nemthor of the Strath-clyde Britons (" de Britannis Alcluidentibus," Tr. Th., 117, c. I.), and that the palace of the prince of that region, daily frequented by Patrick's foster-mother, described by Jocelyn as "in quodam promontorio supereminenti præfato oppido Nemphor" (Tr. Th., 66, c. xi.), was in Ailclyde (Tr. Th., 119, c. xv.).

The Tripartite also has the Armorican story, substantially as told by Probus and the Scholiast on *Fiacc;* and, on the subject of Patrick's continental travels, follows the *Fiacc* in making Patrick's escape from captivity a first step in his continental journey. "Patricio in solitudine agenti, apparuit Angelus, jubens ut in Italiam ad discendas scripturas se conferat. Dixit, propera: ecce nuvis tua parata est" (Tr. Th., 120, c. xxii.). And in equal disregard of the authority of the *Confessio* it puts the call in the islands of the Terrene Sea. As bearing on the question of epoch, it differs from all the antecedent Lives in extending Patrick's period from his first arrival in the 5th of Leoghaire throughout that and the following reign into the 8th year of Lugaid, Leoghaire's son, who succeeded on the death of Ailill Molt, A.D. 481. This brings the death of Patrick of the Tripartite to A.D. 493, the date which has had the acceptance of the greater number of modern writers, these also being of the greater weight. As early indeed as the compilation of the Patrician Synchronismus in the Leabhar Breac (vol. 2, p. 220) which probable associated evidence would refer to the time of Domnall, Archbishop of Armagh, A.D. 1095, this was the received date, and, notwithstanding the evidence of Tirechan to the contrary, it continues to be so in the Annals and in the latest writings of Todd and Shearman. The "Chronicon Scotorum," however, distinguishes A.D. 489 as the date of the death of Patrick the Archbishop and Apostle of the Irish, marking, in nearer accordance with Tirechan, A.D. 457, in the latter part of the reign of Leoghaire, as the obit of "Senior Patrick the bishop, *i.e.* of Glastonbury," a further evidence of the continuing tradition from the time of the writer of the Fiacc Life of there having been at least two Patricks engaged in the Irish mission. But that a missionary of so late a date should have been in living relations with the persons introduced by the Tripartite as Patrick's cotemporaries is very difficult to credit.

XLIV. Amongst the names in the rough index referred to (*sup.* xliii.) is found Saran, son of Coelbadh, and the twelve sons of Coelbadh. Patrick's connexion with them, although not further expanded in the Book of Armagh, is here fully detailed. He desired to found a church at a place not now known in the northern part of Ulster, at that time ruled by Saran, who opposed his wishes. Saran was king of Ulster, in succession to his father, Coelbadh, whose period is the better fixed because he was for one year full king of Ireland, until slain by his successor, Eochaid Muidhmedhon, A.D. 367. This, it will be seen, brings Saran into quasi parity of date with Sinell (*sup.* xxx.), the sons of Cathbod (xxvii.), and Enna Cennsalach (*ib.*) more than half a century before the reign of Leoghaire. The only mode of reconciling these dates with a post-Palladian mission is by supposing that the story of the Tripartite ought to have been told of some other Saran of the same family; and Shearman, in his Dalaradian Descents (Loc. Pat. Tab. 5), passing over the son of Coelbadh, and following the authority of O'Flaherty (Ogyg. iii. c. lxxvii.), has transferred the incident to Saran son of Coelbadh's grandson, Maine.

XLV. But the son of Maine does not appear, like the son of Coelbadh, to have had a brother Nathsluaig, as to whose relations with Patrick the Tripartite is equally explicit as it is in respect of Saran's. Nathsluaig having commended himself to the Saint by an offered donation of land for a church at Coleraine, Patrick accepts the gift in these ambiguous terms: "It shall be mine, yet not cease to be yours; for a grandson of yours as well as of mine shall have his seat and his place of rest therein;" "which language," adds the author, "though it seemed an enigma, yet proved to be a most true oracle; for that bishop *Carbre* who, in this same place, which ever since that day and event is called *Cuil Rathain*, that is, Ferny Close, did afterwards set up his episcopal seat, was grandson of (the same) Nathsluaig, by his son Diguill, in the way of fleshly generation, and likewise in the order of spiritual procreation, was spiritual grandson of the holy Patrick; for bishop Brugach, who is (xvi.) in Rath Mugeonach, ordained bishop by holy Patrick, is he who afterwards ordained *Carbre* bishop" (Tr. Th., 147, 7 a; Vit. ii., c. cxxxvi.), which *Carbre*, it may be observed, is also indirectly noted in the Irish Index (Hog. Doc., 112) as *filius deculli*, in connection with the Coelbadian family. It is hard to read the prediction otherwise than as referring to an event to occur after the deaths of both grandfathers; which would quite agree with what is above observed respecting Coleraine (*sup.* xxv.).

XLVI. The unduly early connexions above mentioned, are balanced in the Tripartite by others equally late as compared with the accepted Patrician epoch. Patrick having made his first convert amongst the Hy-Garrchon of Wicklow, in Sinell, numbered 59, and also his first convert amongst the Dalaraidhe of Down, in Dichu, son of Trechim, numbered 63, returns to the region of Hy-Garrchon, where he receives the hospitality of Killen, and bestows his blessing on Killen's infant son Marcan, being great-grandson of the same Sinell who had been his first convert in the same district (Tr. Th., 152, c. 17). Thence proceeding into the borders of Leix, he escapes the danger of certain pitfalls through the warning of a pious matron, Briga the daughter of Fergnat, son of Cobthac, names of note in the genealogy of the Hy-Ercain or descendants of Ercan grand-uncle of St. Brigid of Kildare (Loc. Pat., Tab. v.). Proceeding thence into northern Munster, he baptizes Eochaid Baldearg, son of Carthen, of the line of Olioll Olum. While Sinell in these Tables of descent is 59 in generation-order, Eochaid is 66, and Briga is 69. Patrick is thus during his missionary career brought in contact with ten successive generations. It might be possible for an individual, in the course of a long life, and under exceptional circumstances, to converse with persons perhaps so far removed in order of birth as the sixth or seventh generation; but there appears no ground for supposing Patrick's ministry in Ireland to have extended through half so great a length of time, much less to have comprised so excessive a range of cotemporaries.

XLVII. Life Six, by Jocelyn of Furness, dates from about A.D. 1185. It relates, in amplified phraseology and not inelegant Latin, the same matters already dealt with, save that it passes by the double series of adventures recorded by Probus; and contributes large additions to the general *actu*, drawn apparently from Tirechan and the Tripartite, or Seventh Life, in reference to which it seems misplaced. So far as concerns this enquiry, it will suffice, to note, that Jocelyn evidently understood Nemthor, or Nemphthor, " Mari Hibernico collimitans" (Tr. Th., 65, c. iv.), to be in North Britain; because, in relating Patrick's journey from the residence of his family towards Gaul, he describes him as "natale solum pertransiens" (Tr. Th., 69, c. xxii.). It contains nothing apposite to the other heads of inquiry not to be found equally at large and probably from earlier sources in the Tripartite, save that (c. 150) it designates Coroticus *Ceretic*, and places him " in finibus quibusdam Britaniæ, quæ modo *Vallia* dicitur," a designation in cotemporaneous use for the Britain of Strathclyde (Chron. Ang-Sax., *passim*).

XLVIII. It is plainly impossible to refer all these incidents, literally as they stand recorded, to a single actor. The reader must either reject such of them as are too early and too late respectively, and refer the residue to the Patrick of popular belief; or else accept the alternative of allocating such of them as appear to stand on an historical basis amongst several Patricks. The former course involves the assumption of a sufficient number of supposed errors of commission and omission in authors and transcribers, to reduce these collateral anomalies to agreement with the body of the *acta*. With these aids, a reasonably consistent account of the Patrick of the Secondary Evidences, in his youth, captivity, continental career, and Irish mission, might be constructed. But if this portraiture be compared with the Patrick of the Primary Evidences, a moral discrepancy, to some minds much more embarrassing than any difficulty of date or person, has to be encountered. For, if the characters presented in the one set of proofs and in the other are to be reconciled, it must be by believing that a conscientious missionary, following in the track of an authorized predecessor, has arrogated to himself all the credit of what had been accomplished by Palladius, if not by Palladius and others; and that a candid student educated in the best schools of the west of Europe should be found lamenting, not only his want of learning, but his want of the opportunities of acquiring it. *Facile potest probari ex saliva scripturæ meæ qualiter sum ego in sermonibus instructus atque eruditus.*

G

XLIX. There seems, therefore, for minds either averse to violent emendations or incapable of reconciling the moral discrepancies in question, no other alternative than to conclude that there were more Patricks than one. On the evidence adduced previously to the considerations now put forward, Dr. Todd had already recognised two— Palladius Patrick, and Patrick Calphurnides; and, since then, Shearman has included with these *Sen* or Senior Patrick of Glastonbury (Loc. Pat., *passim*). Both writers, adhering to the post-Palladian date of all the Patrician *acta*, necessarily ignore the evidences of fourth and early fifth century missionary activity. Both put the mission of Palladius at A.D. 432; but, while Todd fills up the period from thence to 440 with Palladian *acta*, and thence to 493 with those of Patrick, son of Calphurn, Shearman occupies the time from 432 to 463 with the acts of Palladius and of the Glastonbury or old Patrick, and thence to 493 with those of his Third Patrick, the author of the *Confessio*. To allocate the bulk of the *acta* is now impossible; but it is obvious that if events of pre-Palladian times be really predicated of any Patrick in the Lives, they will be more consistently referred to him whose writings have come down to us, and are found to contain no trace of any predecessor in the Irish missionary field.

L. Regarding Patrick's continental travels, there are three schools of opinion traceable in the Lives, these also indicating a growth from traditions respecting several persons. In all, the object is to acquire the knowledge and status necessary for his mission. Muirchu carries him, in the prosecution of this design, no further than Auxerre and Ebmoria; "Fiacc," Tirechan, and the authors of the Second and Fifth Lives conduct him thence to the Terrene Sea islands; and the writers of the Third, Fourth, Sixth, and Seventh Lives and the Scholiast on Fiacc extend his journey onward, expressly or by necessary implication, to Rome. All agree in placing him under the tuition of Germanus, or of Germanus and Martin, which, if he were the missionary cotemporary of Sinell, Saran, Enna, or the elder Dunlang, supposing them to have been rightly marshalled in their dates and pedigrees, could not have been so. These considerations had already led Todd, even while adopting the reading "ex [tra] Gallias" (*sup.* viii., 154 *n.*) to ascribe the major part of these experiences to Palladius, whose family connexions, he has shown, probably allied him with both the ecclesiastics named; and have, doubtless, had their weight in inducing Shearman to the conclusion that whatever portion of the continental record does not belong to the history of Palladius, ought to be divided between the other two, and that, as regards the author of the *Confessio*, his orders at least ought to be deemed altogether British (Loc. Pat., 447; Jour. Arch. Soc. Ir., 258).

LI. As to his place of birth, the preceding analysis of the evidences adds two items only to those already accessible to the eye of criticism; but the evidences, it is believed, are here somewhat more systematically marshalled, and a consideration of them will probably excite surprise that any differences of judgment should have arisen on such premises.

LII. There is greater difficulty in concluding that none of the continental incidents related in the Lives concern the author of the *Confessio*. It is true they attach themselves awkwardly to the story told in the *Confessio* and often contradict it, and in matter and manner are very much below the standard of its reasonableness, dignity, and sincerity; but they are old in compilation, and derived from sources which were old in the beginning of the ninth century; and if they do not relate to the writer of the *Confessio*, certainly do so to some other Patrick or Patricks, so far as their contents can be considered relevant to any one. The existence of an interval of thirty years, during some part of which Patrick was not in Britain (*sup.* viii., 355), between some event not distinctly indicated and some hostile demonstration against the writer, is clearly stated in the *Confessio* (*ib.*, 307). This, if it have not its *terminus a quo* in the fault with which the seniors reproached him (*ib.*), can only, it would seem, be referred to some period of absence from Britain, either for purposes of study or in the prosecution of his mission in Ireland. If the former, his thirty years would tally with the thirty years of continental probation of Muirchu and the other Lifewriters, but would be inconsistent with the probable wants of the student, and with his own disclaimer of educational advantages. If the latter, his language—

"They came . . . they found me after thirty years
To charge me with one word I had confessed
Before I was a Deacon,"

would imply that he had either been followed to Ireland by those who objected to his "laborious episcopate" (*sup.* 127 *n.*), or brought by them before some tribunal in Britain; and the circumstance of his writing with so much warmth of the "dearest friend" who, on that occasion, appears to have taken part adversely to him, would indicate a recent cause of resentment, and perhaps suggest that towards the close of his career his claim to be considered the "Patricius" of the Irish had been called in question.

LIII. Whether there were many Patricks or one, the question of the epoch of the writer of the *Confessio* remains. It will depend in great measure on the mental constitution of the reader, whether he will incline to accept the post-Palladian or the pre-Palladian epoch. In presence of the general agreement of the Life-writers, many may be disposed to lay the primary documents aside as contributing matter only of moral idiosyncrasy, and will reject or adjust collateral divergencies conformably to a mission after A.D. 432. Those minds which find more difficulty in the reconcilement of moral discrepancies will, in adopting the alternative view, rest content with the places assigned in the evidences to the sons of Cathbod, Enna, Sinell, Natsluaig, and Saran, and will allow the balance in which the periods of Coroticus, Fiacc, and Dunlang remain suspended to incline to the side having, in their estimation, the moral preponderance. To judge of these elements of opinion, it was necessary that both sets of evidence should be before the reader, and they are now, it is believed for the first time, presented in one catenation.

LAYS OF THE WESTERN GAEL.

*Cloth, with Portrait of Sir Samuel Ferguson, 2s. ;
Paper Covers, 1s.*

OPINIONS OF THE PRESS.

"THE work of Sir S. Ferguson needs no commendation, but the enterprise of the Irish firm who have undertaken the publication in a cheap form deserves the highest praise. The volume is in fact worthy of universal patronage, and the price is within the reach of all."—*Ulster Gazette.*

"The publication of Sir Samuel Ferguson's works in a cheap and handy form continues. To the 'Hibernian Nights' Entertainments' succeeds the 'Lays of the Western Gael,' and we could desire no better selection from the poet's writings for introduction to a popular audience. He has more of the magic and grace that characterised the works of the older bards; while in no other writer is the Gaelic spirit so strong. His work was not imitative—it was a revival; and when he touches upon topics of his own invention his verse has not less of the Celtic tone. In its treatment of nature it suggests Wordsworth; but there is in it the Celtic magic besides. Now that such excellent and such thoroughly Irish literature has been placed within the reach of modest purses, we trust that it will be widely read by our countrymen. If they wish to know the way in which their fathers thought, and felt, and lived, they could turn to no better guide than Samuel Ferguson. We once more heartily commend the project which has placed such sound, wholesome, and inspiring works within easy reach of the Irish people."—*Nation.*

"'Lays of the Western Gael,' a volume of poems by the late Sir Samuel Ferguson, the eminent antiquary and archæologist, the cultured *littérateur*, and learned scholar. Sir Samuel was above all a poet, and the poetry which he has left us is of that character which fails not to stir the deepest emotions of his readers. These old Irish stories presented in such pleasing ballad form should be read by all who cherish our ancient bardic literature."—*Kilkenny Moderator.*

BY THE SAME AUTHOR.

CONGAL,
A POEM IN FIVE BOOKS. PRICE 7s. 6d.

"The best and greatest work that Sir Samuel Ferguson has left us."—*Blackwood.*

"We are not aware of any requisite quality of a great heroic poem which it does not possess. It is the production of an imagination of the highest order."—*Dublin University Magazine.*

"One of the works in recent poetic literature worthiest of being known and studied."—*Frazer's Magazine.*

"As a poem *Congal* is unquestionably one of the finest products of Irish genius. In the curious felicity of its diction without rudeness, and in the swing of sonorous verse without artificiality or affectation, it has no rival since Chapman's 'Homer.' Sir Samuel Ferguson has worthily crowned a literary life, so brilliantly begun, with a noble and conscientious work, which will illustrate his country's genius as well as his own."—*Catholic World.*

"No poem so Homeric in the march of the narrative, in the character of the heroes, or in the resonant majesty of the versification, has appeared in our time, and withal it is thoroughly and in essence Celtic."—*The Poetry of Sir Samuel Ferguson, by Mr. Justice O'Hagan.*

"*Congal* has the Homeric felicity of descriptive epithet so difficult to re-produce in the more direct phraseology of the Anglo-Saxon speech. Measured purely by the literary standard, the merits of Ferguson's poetry are as strongly marked and distinct as they are high. Not only does the spirit of Celtic Ireland dwell completely and perfectly in his poetry, but I know of no other instance in literature in which such a work has been so thoroughly and successfully accomplished."
—*Alfred M. Williams, Providence, U.S.A.*

POEMS. 7S. 6D.

"Thus traversing all the ages, from the shadowy gigantic forms, and mystic lays of the earliest epoch down to our own times, may we not say that Sir Samuel Ferguson has achieved a great work for his country? If a distinctive National Irish literature in the English tongue, is an achievement of which the foundations have been already laid, then to Sir Samuel Ferguson may the greater praise belong. Be this the pillar of his fame."—*The Poetry of Sir Samuel Ferguson, by Mr. Justice O'Hagan.*

"The characteristics of Sir Samuel Ferguson's poetry, aside from its nationality, are a remarkable strength of rhythm, a happy boldness of epithet, and broad touches of description, that rival Campbell's most powerful effects. It is thoroughly manly in spirit and expression, and its lyrical faculty is frequently of the sort that touches the nerves."—*The Poets and Poetry of Ireland.*

Hibernian Nights' Entertainments

First, Second and Third Series, 1s. *each.*

"These books are capital reading."—*Truth.*

"Much of his best work is embodied in this admirable series of tales."

"The genius, the imaginative grasp, and intimate acquaintance with the habits, customs, history and traditions of Ireland, are all evidenced in these early compositions."—*Southern Advertiser.*

"This fascinating work."—*Morning News.*

"Capital reading."—*Scotsman.*

"It is unnecessary now to speak of the characteristics of Ferguson's prose works. His reputation has long since been established, and though he is known above all as a poet, he will certainly hold a very high position as a narrative writer. He shows in his stories that great knowledge of Celtic life and manners for which he was famed, and besides giving that distinctively Irish local colouring, which is one of the chief merits and charms of his poems, adds the attraction of a singularly pleasing and graceful prose style."—*Cork Examiner.*

DUBLIN : SEALY, BRYERS & WALKER,
94, 95 & 96 MIDDLE ABBEY STREET.

LONDON : G. BELL & SONS,
5 YORK STREET, COVENT GARDEN, W.C.

www.ingramcontent.com/pod-product-compliance
Lightning Source LLC
Chambersburg PA
CBHW020113170426
43199CB00009B/517